'Voices' Memories From a Medium's Life

'Voices' Memories From a Medium's Life

Fiona Roberts

Winchester, UK
Washington, USA

First published by Sixth Books, 2013
Sixth Books is an imprint of John Hunt Publishing Ltd., Laurel House, Station Approach,
Alresford, Hants, SO24 9JH, UK
office1@jhpbooks.net
www.johnhuntpublishing.com
www.6th-books.com

For distributor details and how to order please visit the 'Ordering' section on our website.

ISBN: 978 1 78099 720 9

A CIP catalogue record for this book is available from the British Library.

Design: Stuart Davies

Printed and bound by CPI Group (UK) Ltd, Croydon, CR0 4YY

We operate a distinctive and ethical publishing philosophy in all
areas of our business, from our global network of authors to
production and worldwide distribution.

CONTENTS

Chapter One   1

Chapter Two   8

Chapter Three   15

Chapter Four   26

Chapter Five   35

Chapter Six   41

Chapter Seven   59

Chapter Eight   67

Chapter Nine   72

Chapter Ten   80

Chapter Eleven   86

ALSO BY FIONA ROBERTS:

'GHOST OF A SMILE' – MEMORIES FROM A
MEDIUM'S LIFE

'A BEARD IN NEPAL'
&
'A BEARD IN NEPAL 2. RETURN TO THE VILLAGE'

Keep up to date with Fiona Roberts' books at:
www.spanglefish.com/fionaroberts

Chapter one

The rabbit had been hit by the car travelling in front of us.

We rounded a bend and saw the tiny creature in the middle of the road ahead; it was surely just a baby rabbit, shakily struggling to pull itself along, its shattered back legs dragging uselessly behind it.

The car that had hit it, its occupants then abandoning the injured animal to its lonely fate, was already far off down the coastal road, driving at speed through the remnants of the chilly, early morning mist that drifted in from the sea.

It was around 7am on a Saturday, and I was a front seat passenger in a car driven by my then husband, Billy Roberts. We were heading for Liverpool, and had only just left our house on the outskirts of Southport to drive the twenty five or so miles south, down the undulating, and constantly subsiding coast road.

There was no question of our driving past. How could we?

We stopped, and I hurriedly got out of the car and ran back along the road. There were no other cars around, and through my panic I was grateful it was a weekend, and grateful that Saturday's habitual shopping exodus had not yet started, filling that road with car after speeding car, all intent on reaching the shopping centre car parks in the town.

The little rabbit had stopped moving when I reached it, unable to find the strength to pull itself further across the road. Without a doubt the next car to come round the bend would hit it........

I stooped and picked the small body up in both my hands as gently as I could. It lay silently unmoving, breathing quickly, doubtless terrified, doubtless already near death.

I ran back to the car, trying to hold my hands steady in front of me, trying to keep the rabbit still. I had some idea of driving fast to the nearest vet's surgery – maybe something could be done to save the creature, to quell its pain.

We started off down the road as quickly as its uneven surface would permit, our old car bumping uncomfortably, and rattling along. The small rabbit lay motionless across my hands. Its fur felt warm and soft. There was no external sign of the internal trauma it must surely be suffering - no blood, no marks on the seemingly perfect little body.

We turned off the coast road heading for the town centre and the nearest vet's surgery that we could think of. We drove in silence, each of us submerged in the overpowering agony of helplessness. For we were indeed completely helpless, unable to do anything at all but watch this small creature's final moments in this life.

When the end came, marked by a high pitched call and sudden, violent twitch of the little body, we sat in awful, stunned silence, horrified and distressed to have witnessed this unjust passing.

Billy had stopped the car on double yellow lines not far from the local Police Station, and now two policemen, wondering what we were doing, approached us. They opened the passenger door and saw the small body lying across my hands,

"Could you check that he's dead?" I asked them through my tears, "Just in case."

The policeman reached into the car and carefully lifted the little rabbit from my hands,

"Yes," he said his voice gentle, "I'm sorry luv, but he's gone. He's only a baby, isn't he?" and he laid the rabbit gently back down on my knees.

We turned the car round and drove back home in stunned silence.

I knew I would have to bury the little body in our back garden, so I carried him inside the house and wrapped him in an old, clean, linen tea towel. His soft fur was damp in patches where my tears had fallen on him, and he still felt warm.

Our back garden was pretty big, and was in several places substantially overgrown. Although I tried, I never seemed to have enough time at that point in my life to dedicate to its care. The one really good thing about the garden then was that my father had just paid for solid wooden fencing to be erected all around it, and it was now, as a result, totally enclosed and private. Although we had neighbors' gardens on each side of us, there was a large recreation and sports field at the bottom of all our gardens, so none of us were overlooked at the back of the houses.

The sun was shining that early spring day, and it was pleasantly warm as I dug a hole under the large, spreading bushes in the centre of the garden. Their branches reached eight, maybe ten feet skywards, throwing cool shadows around and about on the grass beneath them. I don't remember what kind of bushes they were, I don't think I ever knew, but they used to be covered in multitudes of pretty white flowers in the springtime. The flowers were perfumed too, and their pleasant aroma often filled the air around the middle of the garden, washing over you unexpectedly if you walked past the bushes.

It was a good place, maybe even a fitting place to bury a small rabbit.

I struggled to make the hole as deep as I thought it should be. The ground was hard and had probably never been dug before, and my old, heavy, second hand spade had seen better days.

Eventually I stood back, wondering if I'd done enough. Yes, that would do nicely I decided. I turned and looked over at the small bundle of old, white linen that lay on the grass a few feet behind me. I had a sudden, overwhelming desire to unwrap the tea towel and check that the little rabbit was still there, that he was still dead. Maybe it was all a mistake? Maybe he was alive and just stunned?

But I knew these thoughts for what they were – a natural

3

human reaction to the trauma of a death.

I picked the bundle up and stood for a moment cradling it, looking down at the newly dug hole. Softly, I told the little rabbit that I was so sorry his life had ended as it did, and I wished him well in his new life in the unseen world beyond.

Then I knelt and carefully placed the bundle in the hole. The linen had been warmed by the sun as it lay on the grass, and I found this warmth somehow comforting as I placed the small, wrapped body into the dark coldness of the freshly dug grave.

I stood up, and for a long time just stared down at the pile of soil I knew I would have to fill the hole with. It seemed such a final act. I didn't want to do it.

But eventually I stooped, and with my hands pushed the soil in on top of the little bundle, covering it, and filling the hole to the top. It was done.

I noticed that the flowers on the bushes above the small grave were almost in bloom; I could just about smell their perfume. Spring was in the air.

"Yes," I thought, "this is a fitting place for a little rabbit."

I went back into the house, and shortly after we got into the car again and drove down to Liverpool.

We collected Billy's son Ben (from one of Billy's previous marriages), and brought him back to Southport to spend the weekend with us. Ben was around the age of six or seven at that time, and living with his mother.

We made no mention to him, or in front of him, of the tragedy that had caused us to arrive late in Liverpool. Ben was a sensitive youngster.

By the time we reached our house again it was raining, and it continued to rain heavily throughout that day and into the evening. It was still drizzling the next morning, but brightened up in the early afternoon.

Having been trapped inside the house for twenty four hours by the bad weather, with little to amuse him, Ben was bored, and anxious to get out into the garden and spend some time wandering around and playing there. As soon as the rain stopped he rushed outside.

I was in the kitchen when he came back in some time later. He ran up to me and said excitedly,

"Come and see the rabbit!" and he pulled at my hand, laughing, trying to drag me over to the door with him.

"What rabbit?" I asked, startled, wondering if he'd somehow managed to see over the new fence. Maybe one of the neighbors had a rabbit in a hutch, "Where is it?" I said, curious.

"In the garden," he told me, "Come and look," and he pulled my hand harder.

I started to walk towards the door, Ben running ahead of me, looking back over his shoulder,

"Come on! Quick!" he pleaded, "It'll go. You'll miss it!"

I reached the door and stepped outside. Ben had run into the middle of the garden and was dashing around, looking left and right, up and down.

"Which garden did you look into?" I called to him, wondering as I said it how on earth he had done that. I couldn't see any way this small child could have seen over a six foot high fence.

"*Here*!" he shouted, "*This* garden. The rabbit's *here*; it's in *this* garden!" and he rushed round the back of the high, spreading bushes in the centre of the lawn.

I suddenly knew what was happening. I *knew* what Ben had seen.

When he came running back a minute later he was disappointed, almost accusing,

"It's gone," he said miserably, "You've missed it."

"What did the rabbit look like, Ben?" I asked him, trying to keep my voice steady.

"Like rabbits always look when they're in the fields," he said, grinning at me, "It was light brown color."

"So it wasn't a grey rabbit like you've got at school, or black like your friend's got at home?" I asked, "Not the same color as those rabbits?"

"No!" Ben said, "I told you, it was a rabbit that lives in the fields. But it was really small, like a baby rabbit."

I smiled. I felt exhilarated, uplifted, as if I had been touched by an angel.

"It just hopped past me over here," and Ben pointed to the area in the middle of the garden, around the bushes, "but it must have got out somewhere, 'cos it's not here now," he said sadly, "I wanted you to see it."

We had never seen any wild rabbits in the garden. We had never seen any on the recreation field behind the house either. We had occasionally seen hedgehogs wandering through the garden, but now that the new fencing had been erected even the hedgehogs couldn't get in. The fences fitted snugly, leaving no gaps anywhere for any visiting wildlife to use.

I knew that Ben had seen the little rabbit I'd buried under the bushes.

Young children are able to see through the veil between this world and the next. Many a time a child may look unknowingly straight into the Spirit World, because through a child's eyes the material and the Spirit Worlds blend seamlessly.

It doesn't occur to a child that what they are seeing, whether human or animal, may no longer have an existence in the material world.

It never ceases to amaze me that an adult, one who believes implicitly in the existence of a life after death, and in the Spirit World, should question the probability of the continued existence of an **animal** after death.

An animal which has known the love of a human is thereby given the possibility, after death, of a continued individual existence in the Spirit World. Yes, your beloved pet, whether dog, cat, horse, no matter what, will live on. You will be reunited.

Those animals which do not live so closely with humans in a material existence, and which may indeed never have had any contact at all with a human being, return after death to their own dimension, and blend once again into the combined soul from which they originally came.

There is no such thing as the state or condition of death, either for a human or for an animal. Death is only a transition from one form of existence to another, different form of existence, and a return to the place from whence we came.

I believe that the little rabbit, when Ben saw him, had stopped for a moment in the garden in order to be noticed, maybe as a thank you for kindness rendered to him. But it would have been a moment's pause only, in this material world, before he began his journey home to that dimension where he would once again blend with the combined soul of the animal kingdom.

Chapter Two

I cannot look back on my childhood and smile. I have no fond memories of time spent with family, doing happy family things together. We didn't do family things, my parents, my brother and myself, and did very little, if anything at all, together.

My father was a strict, unfeeling disciplinarian, whose zeal in that respect was fuelled by his only friend, the whisky bottle. From the first time I saw him, when he came home on leave from sea, I was afraid of him.* (* See 'Ghost of a Smile' for a much fuller explanation.)

However, I do have very fond memories of the time I spent with my maternal grandparents. My Gran had a wicked sense of humor, and Grandy (my grandfather) was not averse to a good chuckle now and again.

As a child I would seek refuge with my grandparents when times were bad at home, and would spend hours playing board or card games with Gran, or asking her about her childhood. She always had something interesting to tell me.

The first spirit person I can recall seeing was at the age of about four, when a 'woman in black' appeared in my bedroom.

It was a very brief visitation, and apart from the fact that the woman was wearing Victorian-type clothes, had her grey hair pulled back into a bun, I think, and had what could be described as a 'severe' face, with deep lines etched into it, I did not glean much more information before she vanished. However, as she faded back into the Spirit World a woman's voice called out, loud and clear, "Aunty May."

I concluded that this woman, who had appeared seated on the edge of my bed, was indeed called Aunty May, and was probably *my* Aunty May. But at that time I did not know who Aunty May was; I had not heard the name mentioned by any adult, and there were no photos around the house resembling the woman I had seen.

My mother was never comfortable with 'the things I saw and heard' as a child, so I judged it prudent, even at that tender age, not to ask her who Aunty May had been.

So it came as something of a shock when, not long after 'the woman in black' appeared to me, my mother began comparing me to 'Aunty May'.

She would say such things as,

"You're just like your Aunty May," or, "Your Aunty May was odd too."

There would always be more than a hint of a sneer in my mother's voice, and she would roll her eyes heavenwards, as if justifiably seeking divine intervention, as she made these comments.

I cannot now recall exactly what it was that I used to say to my mother that provoked the 'Aunty May' jibes from her; I presume I simply told her what I could see or hear on any particular occasion, probably not realizing that **she** could not see or hear the same thing.

Looking back now I know that my mother must have been afraid of the things I said. But she handled my embryonic clairvoyance and psychism badly, for which, however, I cannot blame her. There is nothing so frightening as something we do not understand, particularly if it is something which we cannot see or hear; and my mother's solid, middle class background would not have permitted her to seek out any help or support for such an 'embarrassing' problem as mine – embarrassing to **her**, that is - for my mother always had one eye on what the neighbors would think.

It was my Gran who told me that I was not the only one in the family to have 'the sight'. At least two other members of the family were referred to as 'fey', an old Scottish word meaning clairvoyant, psychic, or able to predict the future. I became number three, after my father's mother, and Aunty May.

Gran told me fascinating stories about my paternal grand-mother's 'doings', as she put it rather dryly. Gran had known her since they were children together. Grannie, as I called my father's mother, was a complex, difficult character, who could start a brawl in an empty room, and often did. She was, however, strongly clairvoyant, and some of the incidents evidencing this clairvoyance became folk law in our family.

In my first book, 'Ghost of a Smile', I set out in some detail the events surrounding the sinking of the ship my father was sailing on, in 1942. His mother 'saw' exactly what happened on that tragic night, and she 'saw' how my father escaped from the torpedoed and sinking ship; she was actually there, and witnessed everything from the 'vehicle' of her astral body. She had travelled astrally, spontaneously, to be near my father in that time of great trauma for him.

This is not such an uncommon event as you may imagine, and there are many well documented examples of spontaneous astral travel, which usually occur when a loved one is in mortal danger.

The 'woman in black' was, I think, my first encounter with a spirit. I remain convinced that Aunty May appeared to me that day in my bedroom in order to reassure me that I was not completely alone in the misery of my childhood, and that others in the Spirit World were watching my life unfold, and were ready to offer support.

Because I was too afraid of my mother's disapproval to ask **her** who Aunty May had been, later on in my life I once again turned to Gran for the information.

"Aunty May?" she said, sounding surprised, "Don't you know who she was?"

"No," I said, "was she **my** Aunty?"

"Sort of," Gran said, "she was Grandy's older sister. So she was your great aunt."

"What was she like?" I asked, settling more comfortably into one of the overstuffed armchairs in Gran's living room.

It was my favorite room in the house; I loved its French windows that opened out onto the small garden. Across the lawn you could see the miniature pond, surrounded by old, strangely shaped flag stones that stood up in places like jagged teeth around the pond's perimeter. This was the pond that my brother had once fallen into as a curious toddler, many years before.

And at the far side of the garden, against the fence, stood a delightful summer house. It probably measured no more than ten feet by eight, and it was no higher than the top of the garden fence, but that little wooden house with the green painted shutters, had provided me with the best of times in my otherwise drab and unfulfilling childhood. I loved it, and had spent many summer nights sleeping on the smooth wooden bench inside, and many summer days watching the garden birds playing in the pond, through the summer house's small windows.

"Your Aunty May was a bit strange," Gran said, smiling almost apologetically at me, "She was fey, you know, and I think quite a few people were afraid of her because of that. My mother used to tell me things about her, odd things May had said to her."

"When did she die?" I asked.

"Well, she was much older than Grandy...." Gran paused, thinking, "She must have been born around the 1880s, and I know she was in her late sixties when she died...."

We sat in thoughtful silence for a few moments. A light breeze crept in through the open French windows, bringing the smell of lavender with it. Gran's lavender plants always did really well, year after year, growing as they did in a sunny, sheltered spot just outside the door.

I suddenly knew that Aunty May was with us. She was there in the room, listening, watching. She had brought the unmistakable smell of lavender with her to my bedroom when she had appeared to me that day, many years ago, and I just knew that she was back again. I could feel her presence.

"May trained as a teacher - she was a very modern woman for her time," Gran continued, "and I think she was a really good teacher too, very conscientious. She was clever and quite witty, and very well read. She usually had a couple of books on the go, and the house was always full of them."

"Was she married?" I asked.

Gran nodded, "Yes," she said, "but her husband died young. It was very sad, and May was never the same again after she lost him." A shadow crossed Gran's face, and she looked away from me, back down the years, remembering. Then she said, "**He** was a teacher too, May's husband George. He was full of fun, always laughing about something or other. He was popular with the other teachers as well as the school children. They seemed a good couple together, he and May, with lots in common", Gran sighed, and shook her head slowly as the memories raced back.

"But George never shared May's fascination with 'strange' things, and with life after death, that sort of subject, the kind of thing **you're** interested in," Gran smiled at me, "I don't think he even believed in an afterlife." She paused, and glanced out the window at the garden. The afternoon sunlight threw restless shadows across the grass and onto the surface of the pond, where the light breeze gently rippled the shallow water. It was a lovely, secluded, peaceful garden.

"Eventually, little by little, May started saying things to people, and frightening them," Gran went on, "telling them about the future, and the past; warning them to avoid certain streets at certain times; not to eat various foods for fear of dire consequences; where to look for something that had been lost, that kind of thing, you know. And then she began talking about 'the dead' to anyone who'd listen. So, obviously, she started to get a reputation as a bit of an oddity. But what frightened people most, of course, was that she was usually right in what she said, and in the predictions she made. Things **did** come true.

But the family just used to laugh, no matter what she said; I don't think any of them took her seriously, at least, not until George died.

I do remember hearing that May's predictions had caused some bad feeling between the couple, and that George was less than pleased with her 'ridiculous utterings', as he called them," Gran paused and grinned at me, "and then May took up with a group of people who were interested in what Arthur Conan Doyle was doing then."

"You mean she got interested in Spiritualism?" I said, surprised, "It was causing quite a stir at that time, wasn't it?"

"Yes," Gran said, "and May would hold forth about it any chance she got! She was fascinated by it. But you know, the family still took no notice of her!"

We both laughed.

"It was my mother who told me what happened next," Gran said, her expression becoming serious, "One day May told George not to go out. He was due to attend a meeting of some sort near the Liver Building in Liverpool. I remember that particularly because the Liver Building had only just been built, but I'm not sure what year it was. Anyway, May told George that she had had a premonition that something catastrophic would happen to him if he went out to the meeting. You can just imagine how George reacted to that! Of course, he wouldn't listen to May. She pleaded with him, she cried, she begged, but all to no avail. George went out to the meeting.

Later that same day May went round to her parents' house. I think they still lived in Walton, Liverpool, at that time. When her mother answered the door she was shocked to see May standing there on the doorstep, dressed completely in black.

"What's happened?" she said anxiously to her daughter, "What on earth's happened?"

"It's George," May said simply, and she stepped into the house and made her way to the small, cluttered living room, where she sat down and waited in silence, refusing absolutely to speak to anyone, or to explain what was happening.

The knock on the door came a couple of hours later. One of George's friends stood pale and shaken on the doorstep. He had been with George at the meeting, and slowly and quietly he told May what had happened. George had had a sudden heart attack, and died instantly.

"May was never the same after that," Gran said, "understandably, I suppose. I think she wore black every day for the rest of her life. Mind you, even if she'd persuaded George not to go to the meeting, he would still have died; he would still have had the heart attack. But my mother always thought that May somehow blamed herself for George's death. Perhaps May felt that if she'd stopped him going out he wouldn't have died."

A silence fell between us. A blackbird sang suddenly and beautifully outside on the grass.

"Did she get involved in Spiritualism, I mean, **more** involved in it, after George died?" I asked after a moment.

"No," Gran said, "she didn't. I'm not sure why, but she didn't. Apparently she still used to tell people strange things, and friends and neighbors would ask her for advice sometimes, but that's all."

I wish I had met Aunty May in this life. I wish I had been able to sit down and talk to her. I'm sure I would have liked her.

Chapter Three

There must be very many of us who have been shocked into wakefulness by the crystal clear sound of a voice calling our name. Just that, and no more. Just a name, called out so clearly that the voice could have come from someone standing beside our bed, or leaning over our sleeping form.

For most people, once the initial shock of such a rude awakening has receded, there is a tendency to dismiss the incident as 'just a dream', or 'just my imagination playing tricks'. Well, maybe. But then again, maybe not.

The point at which the physical body enters or leaves the sleep state is well known as a point at which the Spirit World may often manage to make us aware of their presence. For we are, at this time, 'open' or susceptible to the vibrations of another dimension.

Under normal circumstances, in the living of our everyday lives, for most people the 'voices' from the Spirit World fall on 'deaf' ears, no matter how persistent those 'voices' may be.

Our consciousness drives us through the daily business of living, keeping us focused on any number of mind consuming, pressing material duties, leaving no gaps in that consciousness through which a signal, or communication from another dimension may penetrate.

The 'voices' which many of us may hear upon waking or falling asleep, will not be audible to maybe 99% of us during the course of a normal day. Our ears, our senses, are not attuned to the sounds of another dimension. We live in this, our material world, and our senses are firmly attuned here, to this world, and not to the spiritual realms.

This is as it should be. There is a time and a place for everything.

The Spirit World, however, would seem to have other ideas

where communication is concerned, and their dogged persistence at making their presence felt will, on occasions, pay off for them. Some of us will hear 'voices' at inappropriate, even intrusive moments.

Of course, communication is the name of the game, isn't it? And I would hazard a guess that most people would give their eye-teeth to hear a spirit voice, or some other clearly discernible sound emanating from the realms of the Spirit World. We desperately want that elusive evidence, that proof of a continued existence of the human spirit, the human consciousness, after death.

But few people do anything at all to facilitate spirit communication, and even fewer people seem to be aware that for communication to be successful, it has to be worked at, honed, and refined, usually over quite a number of years.

I wish I had one penny for every time a client has said to me something along the lines of,

"I haven't heard my husband's voice at all since he died. If there really **is** a Spirit World, and if he's there and alive, I know he'd be speaking to me, telling me he's fine."

Well, he very probably **is** speaking to her, telling her he's fine, but **she** is simply not equipped to **hear** his spirit voice. Why would she suddenly be able to receive communication from the Spirit World, when she never has before? The passing of a loved one does not instantly equip those left here in the material world to be able to receive spirit communication, no matter how much they would like that.

We are all born into this life with some kind of psychic ability, to some greater or lesser extent, but the majority of the population never recognize their psychic self, and never acknowledge or use it in any conscious way.

Being 'psychic' may manifest in a variety of guises. Intuition, the sure and certain feeling that, for example, 'something is wrong', or '**someone** is wrong', or 'this situation is not safe', is a psychic ability. My Grannie apparently used to say she could 'feel it in her water' if something untoward was going to happen! More often than not she was right.

But try to analyze that feeling, to pin it down and define it, and you simply can't. Psychic abilities are easier to accept than to explain, although there are now some very comprehensive books on the subject.

Throughout my life I have heard 'voices'. As a child I grew used to waking suddenly, with the sound of a perfectly clear voice calling my name still ringing in my ears; and on many occasions I was startled by a sudden, single loud shout as I reached a certain point on my way down the stairs in my parents' house.

I was never afraid; I knew instinctively that these were the voices of those in the Spirit World, but I was curious. I wanted to know why they were calling to me, and what they wanted to tell me, if anything.

However, only very rarely does anything else, any **other** communication, follow the spontaneous, unexpected voice that calls out from the Spirit World. Why is that? Well, maybe this phenomenon is designed to test whether the spirit voice is heard by its intended recipient; or maybe it is simply a form of greeting, a happy acknowledgement that life does indeed continue beyond the bounds of our physical vision, and our physical senses.

That is not to say that other, more **meaningful** spirit communication does not occur under different, more controlled circumstances – of course it does.

I never had the opportunity of speaking to my father's mother about her 'gift'. She lived in an uncomfortable world of spats and arguments with neighbors and family; of slights and perceived slights from acquaintances; of disagreements with trades people; and fallings out with my father and mother.

I remember going to Grannie's house maybe only six or seven

times in my life, although I grew up living just round the corner from her.

In later years, when my father and I were reconciled, he told me many things about his family that I hadn't known, and many things about Grannie's life that I would otherwise never have discovered. Those years, the last years with my father, were filled with fascinating revelations.

Grannie also heard 'voices' throughout her life. One day Dad told me this:

He remembered, as a child, being roundly told off on numerous occasions when Grannie had stopped what she was doing downstairs, and traipsed upstairs to see what he wanted, wondering why he had called her, which of course he **hadn't**.

Adding insult to injury, she would occasionally berate him for calling her 'Ella' (her name) instead of 'Mum', when (as **she** thought) he had called downstairs to her.

Dad knew about the voices that Grannie heard; he had grown up knowing, and was never in the least bothered about them, so he didn't take these tellings off to heart and, importantly, he learned not to smile or make any comment during them. For such actions were regarded by his mother as no less than red rags to a bull, and were ample excuse to set her off in a ranting rage.

So he didn't pay all that much attention when Grannie asked him one day who 'Alexander' was. He simply told her that he didn't know anyone of that name.

Dad was about twelve years old when the 'Alexander' incident occurred. He and his parents had just moved to a pleasant house in a quiet, northern suburb of Liverpool, and were still settling in there.

But the next day Grannie asked again,

"Are you sure you don't know anyone called Alexander? Is there a boy at school, a friend of yours, maybe?" she said, watching my father intently.

"No," Dad said, "I can't think of anyone at all called

Alexander. Why do you ask?"

"Oh, it's not important," Grannie told him, and swiftly changed the subject.

But Dad could see that there was something playing on his mother's mind, and he was curious,

"Is that a first name or a surname?" he asked her.

"Well, I really don't know," she told him in her broad Scottish accent, "I think it might be either."

There was a thoughtful silence, and mother and son looked across the breakfast table at each other. The house seemed very quiet indeed; the only sound came from the stately old grandfather clock that marked time in the cool hallway. Its steady, measured tick tock could be heard from every room in the house. My father loved the sound; he found it strangely reassuring.

The fact that Dad's father, my grandfather, had left Liverpool the day before to return to sea for a number of months, only added to the quiet emptiness in the old house. Sam was a ship's engineer, and the sea was his life, as it would soon become my father's life too.

Dad went to school that day as usual, and gave no more thought to Grannie's questions about someone called Alexander.

When he arrived home that afternoon he was surprised to find the house empty. It was unusual, because his mother always made a point of being home when he came in after school. She insisted on hearing all about his school day, and would check over any homework he had been given. This had been the accepted routine for as long as he could remember.

Dad went into the kitchen and got himself a glass of milk – another routine that his mother insisted on. He carried it into the lounge and sat down on the armchair by the window. This was **his** chair, he rarely sat anywhere else. It was just the right size, just the right firmness for him. He wasn't comfortable on any other chair.

His book lay on the coffee table where he had left it the

evening before. Picking it up, Dad began to read, and was instantly and wonderfully transported onto a ship on the high seas a hundred years before. The thrill and the adventure of man's struggle to survive against the elements engrossed him; he heard the howl of the wind rushing through the rigging, and saw the merciless waves breaking across the ship's bow. Time passed by unnoticed.

It could have been as much as half an hour later when he took a sip of milk and glanced out the window. He saw her immediately. His mother was in the garden.

But he didn't know what she was doing.

Slowly, never taking his eyes off his mother, Dad stood up, placed the glass of milk carefully on the coffee table, and moved nearer to the window. From where he stood he could see the whole garden.

It was quite a large garden, but in Dad's opinion it was boring as gardens went, because it consisted mainly of perfectly shaped, perfectly cut lawn, and little else. Even the slender, neat borders around the lawn were sparsely populated, boasting no more than a daffodil or two at Easter time.

Neighbors' gardens adjoined this one on three sides – left, right, and the end, and there was little to choose between any of them in the attractive gardens category. They were unashamedly middle class gardens in an unashamedly middle class neighborhood.

Grannie was standing at the low fence which divided the neighboring garden on the left from her garden. She was standing stock still, her head cocked to one side, staring into next door's garden, her back towards the lounge window.

"What on earth is she doing?" Dad thought, noticing with dismay that his mother was actually standing on the soil of the garden border, something she would never normally have considered doing. Her shoes were caked in thick, damp soil. He felt a cold shiver of apprehension pass down his spine.

Something must be wrong, but he had no idea what it could be.

Dad raised a hand to knock on the window, thinking to catch his mother's attention, to ask her what she was doing, but before his hand made contact with the glass his mother suddenly walked quickly away, down to the bottom of the garden, her shoes leaving a trail of muddy imprints behind her on the otherwise perfectly green lawn.

Reaching the end of the garden she hardly paused before stepping onto the soil border there, and walking up to the low fence, where she struck the same pose as she had done at the side of the garden a few moments before. Head tilted to one side, as though listening intently, she stood without moving a muscle.

Dad began to think his mother must be ill. He walked quickly out of the lounge and through the hall, past the old grandfather clock standing in the corner, into the kitchen, and out through the back door into the garden. His mother had not moved.

Taking a deep breath, Dad walked steadily across the lawn towards her. As he did so it began to rain. He knew that Grannie hated to get her permed hair wet, and she never went out of the house without her rain hat and umbrella, even on sunny days, so if he needed any more evidence that all was not well, here it was. His mother took absolutely no notice of the rain that now fell heavily onto her unprotected hair.

"Mum!" Dad called, stopping a couple of feet in front of the border, "What are you doing? Is something wrong?" he asked anxiously. His mother, her back to him, did not move, and made no sign of having heard him.

"Mum!" he shouted, beginning to panic, "Mum!"

Suddenly Grannie turned towards him,

"Did you hear that?" she asked somewhat breathlessly, "You must have heard that?"

"What?" Dad said, "Hear what? What are you doing out here? It's raining!" and he reached out to take his mother's hand, thinking to try to lead her back into the house.

"Listen!" she said, "Just listen!" her voice held a strident, strangely unfamiliar tone that frightened my father. He didn't know what to do, and simply stared aghast at her, as the rain steadily soaked both of them.

But Grannie must finally have realized that her distinctly odd behavior was upsetting her son, because a moment later she reached out and took his hand,

"Come on," she said, sounding calmer now, "we're getting wet. Let's go in."

Grannie would not explain her behavior, and she would not answer Dad's questions. Later that evening, when they were both warm and dry, and were settled in the lounge after dinner, Dad tried again,

"What did you hear in the garden?" he asked, "Was it a 'voice'? Did you recognize it? What did it say?"

Grannie raised a hand in Dad's direction, effectively stopping the flow of questions,

"I'm sorry I frightened you," she said, "but we will say no more about it. Don't ask me again."

He knew she meant it. He knew better than to disobey her.

The days passed, weeks, maybe a month. Nothing changed in Dad's life, nothing changed at school, nothing changed at home. He had forgotten about the incident in the garden, and forgotten too about the 'Alexander' incident. His mind was crammed to bursting with Latin declensions, historical dates, and algebra, to the exclusion of all else.

And then one cold, dark October night Dad awoke, sure he had heard a sound in the house, sure it had woken him. He sat up in bed and listened. A chill breeze blew through the old silver birch tree in the back garden, rattling the few dry leaves that still clung to its highest branches, pulling them off where it could, and sending them skidding across the neighbor's lawn to collect in damp piles against the bottom of the wooden fence.

Dad listened, but the house was steadfastly silent, save for the regular tick tock of the old grandfather clock in the hall downstairs. Nothing moved.

Dad's bedroom was over the lounge, and his window looked out onto the garden below. Whenever he could he left the heavy curtains undrawn and the small, top window slightly open at night, the better to see the stars as he lay in bed. He would imagine himself to be on a sailing ship in the middle of a vast ocean, becalmed, and navigating by means of those bright, twinkling stars.

But more often than not he would awaken the next day to find the window shut and the curtains closed, as his mother always secured the house for the night after he was asleep.

Dad got up in the darkness and walked over to the window. He pulled the curtains apart just enough to provide him with a decent, uninterrupted view of the night sky, which on that particular night was well worth seeing.

The light breeze dragged the remnants of the day's heavy rain clouds across the face of the almost full moon, and the garden below Dad's window was in turn washed in pale, silver light, and darkened by patches of irregular, moving shadows.

Dad stood and watched the scene for maybe five minutes before he noticed the figure in the garden.

He was shocked and leant forward, staring intently out the window, hardly breathing. The figure disappeared, enveloped by moon shadow, and then reappeared shining in ghostly guise as the clouds sped away again.

He could not believe his eyes as he watched his mother, wearing her long, cream silk dressing gown and slippers, walking determinedly across the lawn to the fence at the bottom of the garden.

Once again the figure vanished into the passing darkness, and when the moon finally lit the garden again Grannie was standing exactly as she had been that day a month ago, looking over the fence into the neighbor's garden, head cocked, listening to something that only she could hear.

My father was appalled. For a moment he couldn't sort out his jumbled thoughts, but then he did what was probably the best thing to do given the circumstances. He went back to bed.

Of course he couldn't sleep, and lay anxiously listening, hoping to hear his mother come back into the house. The closing of the heavy bolt on the back door made a scraping squeak, loud enough to be heard upstairs, but Dad didn't settle until he heard his parents' bedroom door close softly a few moments later. It was a long time before he drifted into fitful sleep.

Dad decided to think carefully about the situation before saying anything to his mother. She was a difficult person, prone to flying into inexplicable fits of temper at the drop of a hat, and sometimes going many days refusing to speak to anyone.

He would have to approach this tactfully, if at all.

But as it turned out Dad did not have to make a decision one way or the other, because when he arrived home after school the next day the local newspaper had been delivered, and it contained the following facts:

A well known local shopkeeper had been found dead in his shop. It appeared he had committed suicide. The shopkeeper's wife had not been seen for several weeks, and now amid concerns for her safety, a search was underway for her.

My father would not have paid very much attention to this article had it not been for the shopkeeper's name. It was 'Alexander'. Mr Alexander.

When, several days later, the police discovered the body of the shopkeeper's wife buried in the garden of their house, Dad chose his moment, took a deep breath, and then cautiously asked Grannie what, if anything, she knew about it.

This is what she eventually told Dad:

Grannie had heard a woman's 'voice' calling to her from the Spirit World, shouting 'Alexander', again and again. This kind of thing was not unusual, as Grannie often heard spirit voices, but as time went on, and the 'voice' became more insistent, she somehow **knew** that this woman had been brutally murdered.

Grannie became convinced that the woman had been killed, and then buried in a garden.

The spirit 'voice' had been so loud, so clear and persistent, that Grannie began to think the woman was buried in one of her neighbors' gardens, and many times she heard the woman's 'voice' seemingly coming from the other side of her garden fence.

When my father had seen Grannie out in the garden in the middle of the night, she had been awakened by the woman's screams, followed by the loud, agonizing shouting of the name 'Alexander'. Not knowing what else to do, Grannie had run out into the garden, wondering if the poor woman was trying to show her where her body had been buried.

As it turned out the woman's body was found in the garden of her own house, which was quite some distance away from Dad's parents' house.

Grannie would never allow this incident to be spoken of again, and she made my father swear not to tell **his** father, or anyone else about it. Dad was, understandably, happy to comply.

Interestingly enough, my father told me that he had always believed that Grannie had told the police where to look for the unfortunate wife's body. Presumably she had said to them,

"Dig in the garden," rather than, "Dig in my neighbor's garden"! Thereby happily averting what would without doubt have been a dreadful crisis between neighbors!

Chapter Four

Dreaming is a perfectly natural occurrence. There is nothing strange or untoward about the act of dreaming; even animals dream. We may perhaps awake in the morning with our minds full of jumbled impressions, and disquieting memories of saying and doing unfamiliar, odd things during our dreams, but these fragmented mental images quickly drift out of our consciousness and are rapidly forgotten.

Even a particularly vivid dream, one which is seemingly firmly lodged in your memory upon waking; one which may be so noteworthy that you commit it to paper, or tell somebody about it; even **that** dream will not endure in your consciousness. Within days all but the smallest trace of it will have gone, and even re reading your notes will not enable you to recall all of its details to your conscious mind.

This, the psychologists tell us, is how it should be. Simply put, the act of dreaming serves the purpose of removing the potential overload of mental dross which has built up over time, from our consciousness.

However, I am certain that all of us have had at least one dream which, though it may have occurred many years ago, is still as clear in our minds in all its details, as it was the morning after it happened. It very probably featured a person, or people, who we knew to be dead.

That 'dream', the one which you can recall vividly even after such a long time has passed, was not in fact simply a dream. It was an 'astral encounter'.

An astral encounter is exactly as it sounds i.e. an encounter or meeting with someone, maybe human, maybe animal, on the astral planes.

The astral planes are those planes of existence closest in vibration to our material world; they are in fact the 'next step up', so to speak, on the spectrum of vibration; and of course the whole of creation is in constant vibration. Within the universe positive and negative waves of energy are constantly vibrating. Each color that we see has its own frequency, and vibration is responsible for every sound that we hear.

The material or physical world which we inhabit is the lowest on the vibratory scale. The further away we move from our physical world, the faster the vibration, and the more spiritual the realms or planes of existence we encounter.

Hence we speak about Heaven being somewhere 'above', corresponding to a faster rate of vibration, and Hell being somewhere 'below', equating to a much slower rate of vibration.

In fact, Heaven and Hell are not actual places, but are conditions or states of being.

After death, released from the constraints of a physical body which is attuned and adapted to life in a material realm, the freed spirit will naturally gravitate to that plane of existence upon which it feels a compatible vibration. Your spirit, that is, *you*, will 'find its own level' in the afterlife, and will simply not be able to exist comfortably at a level of vibration which is not compatible with its own, be it a higher level or a lower one.

After death we will therefore find ourselves in exactly the **right** place, as we begin our new life on the astral planes.

There are a great many sub divisions within the astral planes, and it is to these dimensions that most human spirits will gravitate after completion of yet another incarnation on earth.

However, in the sleep state our spirit will leave its physical body, and travel in its astral body to the astral planes. Here it will meet (encounter) the spirits of those friends, family and loved ones who have died, and who now have their existence on the astral plane.

Not all astral encounters are well remembered, and on occasion you may awake with vague memories of faces glimpsed, or snatches of conversations with 'lost' loved ones floating somewhere at the back of your consciousness. These fragmented memories will not endure.

But some astral encounters are so precious, so longed for, that they remain fixed in our memory in every detail, retrievable at will, for the rest of our lives.

We have all heard, or maybe even said, something along the lines of:

"I dreamed about my mother last night. It was so real, she looked exactly like she used to. I felt as if I was really speaking to her."

Well, you probably were; and if the memory of that 'dream' stays bright and detailed in your mind year after year, you should perhaps count your blessings, and draw comfort from the realization that you did in fact meet up with your mother on the astral planes.

Throughout all the nine sad and difficult years of my marriage to Billy Roberts, my wonderful, fun loving Old English sheepdog Harry was, when we were not travelling for Billy's work, my constant companion. Without a doubt we loved each other, and his eventual loss affected me deeply.

Harry developed a heart problem when he was about eight years old, and his health gradually deteriorated over the next year. He slowed down, and found walking any distance increasingly difficult. Eventually he couldn't climb the stairs at home, and would sit and cry for me on the bottom step.

As a late, chilly spring turned into summer it began to look as though the end was approaching. I was devastated.

But the end was already very much in sight where my marriage was concerned, and Billy and I had been living separately in the house for a number of months already.

Harry and I had settled into the front room downstairs, and saw little or nothing of Billy, who spent most of his time in Liverpool, with the woman he would eventually move in with.

Days would pass, and he would not come back to the house. I

was glad. I had reached the stage when I had nothing more to say to him, and my thoughts were already on a happier, more fulfilled future without him.

But although I had already made plans for my future, and for a divorce, everything was on hold while I looked after an increasingly weaker Harry.

"He's not in any pain," the vet told me after examining Harry for the umpteenth time, "but I must say I'm really surprised that he's still with us." He smiled rather ruefully, and rumpled Harry's untidy fringe that hung down over his big, startlingly blue eyes. Just looking at Harry had always made people smile. He was that kind of dog.

I put yet another bottle of tablets with the label 'Harry Roberts' on it into my bag, thanked the vet and, having no transport of my own at the time, we got a taxi home. Harry was too ill to walk.

The weather turned warm, and Harry and I spent time together in the garden. I caught up on books that I had been meaning to read for months but never had the time, while Harry lay sleeping on the grass, in the cool shade under the bushes in the centre of the garden.

In the midst of my despair I managed to find an oasis of much needed peace, and gradually the slow process of becoming 'myself' again began.

The past few years had been hectic and tiring as I worked hard at promoting Billy's career as a medium and psychic, and writing books for him.

I had really enjoyed what I did, and learned a great deal about those subjects which had always been such a huge part of my life. I began to wonder what the future held in store for me.

It was at this time that I discovered I was Billy's fourth wife, not third, and that he had two sons from previous marriages, not one.

There are moments in our lives when time itself seems to take a deep breath and stand still, and moments when Universal Law seems to provide us with a ready made opportunity to take stock, and to make plans for the future. We find ourselves at a cross-roads, and the decisions we make then will reverberate throughout the rest of our lives. Such a moment was just around the corner for me. But I knew that I would have to step across the threshold into a new era in my life, without my beloved Harry.

When that dreadful day came, that awful day when I lost him, all the knowledge I had gleaned over the years, everything that I knew for a certainty about the Spirit World, everything I had experienced, everything that I had been privileged to see and hear, counted for nothing at all. For I had lost the physical presence of my faithful companion; and I could **feel** his absence as if that itself were a living thing.

I first met Billy Roberts at a week long Spiritualist workshop /training event in Bournemouth. I sat enthralled during the lectures and workshops that he gave, knowing without a doubt that I was listening to one of the country's most knowledgeable speakers on the subjects of Spiritualism and the Paranormal.

Billy came from Wavertree in Liverpool, and still lived there, whereas although I too came from Liverpool, I was living in Folkestone at the time. (In *Ghost of a Smile*, my first book, I have explained how it was that I came to be living in Kent, and in Paris before that.)

Eventually, after many years away from the city of my birth, I moved back to Liverpool to be with Billy, exchanging the pleasant green fields, valleys and vineyards of Kent for the small backstreet in Wavertree, Liverpool, where he lived. But I didn't care about the environment; at that time I was in love, and every-thing was rosy.

Billy lived in a small house in the middle of a terrace. Each front door opened directly onto the pavement. The short, narrow street, built in a slower, less complicated time of horses and carts, was now barely wide enough for two cars to pass. The wonderful sense of community which had once existed amongst the neighbors there had long since vanished, giving way to surly silence and sullen mistrust, as strangers who lived maybe two doors apart, passed each other without a second glance.

Billy's house was run down and dilapidated, barely recognizable as the house it had once been, and it was quite some time before we managed to afford the necessary renovations. Until then we lived like illegal campers on a building site, stepping around a large hole where the backroom floor had collapsed, and nailing old curtains across doorways, as there was not one single internal door remaining in the property.

Billy's Auntie Sadie lived alone in the house next door. The day we took Harry to meet her she couldn't stop grinning; she loved him from the first time she saw him. He was always a welcome visitor in her house, and he knew it!

Whenever Billy's work took us away from Liverpool, or just out for an evening demonstration of clairvoyance or a workshop, Harry would stay with Sadie. He was like the child that she never had. She loved his company, and loved making a fuss of him.

Sadie's small living room was just about big enough to accommodate two armchairs, a table and a TV, and not much else. Many's the time Billy and I arrived, day or night, to find Sadie snoring gently in one armchair, and Harry curled up and snoring in the other, looking for all the world like an old married couple, content in each other's company.

Even after Billy and I moved to Southport, twenty miles from Liverpool, we would still take Harry to stay with Sadie on a regular basis. They both enjoyed those visits.

Sadie had a heart condition, and a terrible, irrational fear of doctors and hospitals. Sadly, she died a few years before Harry.

Two days after Harry's death I awoke in the morning with the memory of a vivid dream clear and bright in my mind.

That 'dream' was **so** clear, **so** bright, that I knew instantly it had not been simply 'a dream'. I knew with absolute certainty that it had been an astral encounter - I had met up with Harry on the astral planes.

Today, many years later, that astral encounter remains indelibly imprinted on my consciousness, clear and sharp in all its aspects, bright and unblurred in every corner, as if it had happened yesterday.

This is it:

I stood at the end of the short, narrow street in Wavertree, Liverpool, where we had lived for three years. As I looked down towards our old house, and Sadie's house next door to it, I realized that there was something strange about the daylight. It was very bright everywhere, but that brightness was not harsh; it did not make me want to shade my eyes against it. It possessed, in fact, a gentle, serene and calming quality.

Every inch of the scene in front of me was perfectly illuminated; the numbers on the house doors stood out in relief; the ragged cracks in the pavement flagstones seemed magnified, each one completely defined, as if painted in black on the ground; and the light glinted sharply off the surface of the street, revealing the old, worn cobbles there, not tarmac.

But there **was** something unusual about the brightness. I looked up to the sky and saw a vivid blue panorama above me, almost, but not quite the 'normal' blue sky color. The absence of a sun in the sky struck me as odd. I suddenly realized that I could not see any source of the all pervading, calming light, and that not a single shadow was cast anywhere by it.

I stepped onto the street and walked slowly down towards Sadie's house. The absolute, silent stillness was pleasant; there was no one else around either on the pavements or in the houses. I knew I was completely alone.

I stopped in front of Sadie's house and reached out a hand to push the old wooden front door. It seemed to open silently on its own, and I stepped inside.

Everything in the small hallway was exactly as I remembered it. The staircase was immediately in front of me, its carpet worn thin on the first few steps. The paint on the banister was still chipped and flaking at the bottom, and Sadie's raincoat, her favorite, hung across it.

I moved past, my arm brushing the coat and dislodging its belt, which fell with a dull clunk as the buckle made contact with the wood of the banister.

I walked slowly along the narrow hall towards the living room door. As I reached it the door opened and Sadie appeared there, standing in the doorway, one hand resting lightly on the door handle.

She looked exactly as I remembered her; her face, her hair, her skin, nothing was any different, and she was dressed in the same kind of clothes she had always worn in her material existence. I stared at her, waiting for her to speak,

"He's in here," Sadie said, and her voice was unmistakably the same voice that I remembered. She spoke quietly, looking straight at me, and I noticed particularly the expression on her face. It was not a welcoming smile, and there was not even a suspicion of surprise there at my visit, but rather she appeared slightly worried, maybe even anxious, as she stood back to allow me to enter the room.

I stepped across the threshold in front of Sadie and looked to my right. At first I could see nothing at all. The room was completely devoid of light, and I stared into the heavy darkness, waiting. Little by little I began to see the outline of one of Sadie's armchairs. As it became clearer I walked towards it, knowing that this was what I'd come for, this was what I wanted.

I stopped beside the chair and looked down. Harry was asleep there, curled up in the old familiar way, just about fitting onto the chair cushion, one paw hanging over the front edge, inches from the floor.

I stared intently down at him, and reached out to touch his

head, ruffling that ever untidy fringe.

He woke up, and those wonderfully expressive blue eyes of his opened, and met mine.

I felt myself unable to move, emotion seemed to root me to the spot, and things seemed now to unfold in slow motion.

Harry got off the armchair, and I turned and followed him as he walked a little distance away. Then he sat down, and I sat beside him on the floor, as I had done so many times over the years. I put my arms around him and hugged him close, feeling the warmth of his soft, thick fur, smelling the familiar Harry scent, and feeling something of the joy I always used to feel in his presence.

And then I was standing at the living room door again, looking back at Harry still sitting on the floor. Sadie was standing beside him, one hand resting on his head, smiling now in my direction. I could see nothing else around the two of them, only complete darkness, but they stood out vividly, with all the clarity and brightness of a perfectly detailed picture.

I knew my visit was over, and I turned slowly and left the room, closing the door softly behind me.

The details of this astral encounter are as clear in my mind today as when it happened many years ago, and this is of course exactly what makes an astral encounter different from a run of the mill dream, the elements of which do not endure, and are quickly erased from the consciousness.

This kind of occurrence is far from unusual, and brings great comfort to untold numbers of people lucky enough to have experienced an astral encounter.

Chapter Five

I have been fortunate enough to count several astral encounters amongst my experiences, and one in particular stands out as distinctly unusual. Perhaps you will forgive me for recounting it here.

Towards the end of my marriage a number of life changing events and circumstances came together to make that period probably the most difficult of my life.

My parents both became ill – my mother with leukemia, and my father with the wear and tear of old age, exacerbated by an almost lifelong alcohol habit.

They kept the local hospital busy, and were often both in there for treatment at the same time. I did the best I could to support them, to-ing and fro-ing from my house to theirs, while struggling myself with the sometimes seemingly insurmountable problems associated with the ending of a marriage, making a living, moving home, and all that those life changing events entailed.

A number of good friends stood by me, and I knew I could call upon their help if needed. But one in particular proved a veritable tower of strength to me, and was never too busy either to listen to my woes, or provide help of a more practical nature.

I met Carolyn when Billy and I needed advertising posters and flyers made for some of his local events. She ran a business doing just that, amongst many other things. Her boundless energy and attention to detail never ceased to amaze me. Later on she typed up some of the manuscripts for Billy's books, and designed the cover for one of them.

I admired the constant high quality of her work, and the enthusiasm with which she approached even the most mundane of jobs; but above all Carolyn's sense of humor, similar in many ways to my own, appealed to me.

We became good friends, and still are.

Two, maybe three months after Harry's death, I awoke one morning with the sure and certain knowledge that I had met him again. The crystal clear memory of the night's 'dream' replayed like a film across the screen of my consciousness, over and over again.

It was a wonderful, happy 'encounter' featuring not only Harry, but Carolyn too, and it was clear and complete in my memory in all its details.

Here it is:

I stood at the edge of a wide, grassy expanse, beyond which I could see sand dunes, and in the far distance the sea.

I knew the area in which I found myself; I knew it was in Southport, where I lived.

I stood perfectly still, waiting for something. There was a light breeze blowing off the sea – it felt pleasant on my face – and it was warm. Nothing moved within my field of vision; there was no one in sight.

I stared out to sea, watching the bright glints of sunlight playing over the gently shifting water. It felt very peaceful there.

I looked up at the sky and noted the motionless clouds above me. They seemed almost transparent, reflecting the rays from a sun I could not see.

"Hi there!" The voice was pleasantly familiar, and I turned round towards it.

Carolyn was getting out of her car and waving. I waved back, knowing I had been expecting her, pleased to see her.

As she walked over to me I noticed the 'round house', a well known Southport landmark, across the road behind her.

"Where is he?" she asked, smiling, as she reached me. I noticed she was wearing a pink and grey scarf round her neck.

"Over there," I told her, turning and pointing back towards the sand dunes in the distance.

We stood together in companionable silence and waited,

watching.

Suddenly I saw Harry,

"Here he comes!" I shouted, laughing.

Harry came racing over the uneven grassy expanse towards us, his grey and white fur fringe flattened across his face by his speed; mouth open, and tongue out, looking for all the world as if he had a huge grin on his face.

Carolyn and I laughed and ran to meet him, and then the three of us raced each other up and down the sand dunes, stumbling, falling on the soft sand, screeching with laughter; and all the while Harry barked with excitement and joy.

When eventually we sat down on the gently sloping side of a dune, all three of us puffing and panting, and Carolyn and I still laughing, she said,

"What about a 'Mivi'?"

"Yes!" I said, "I'd love a lolly ice, but it's got to be a **strawberry** Mivi!"

"OK, let's have strawberry Mivis!" Carolyn said.

We sat together, the three of us, and Carolyn and I enjoyed our strawberry lolly ices. They were good.

The air was warm and pleasant, the view was peaceful, and we were happy.

Then we said good bye to Harry until the next time, secure in the knowledge that there would be a next time, and watched as he raced away from us across the grass and into the sand dunes in the distance. In an instant he had vanished from our view.

You may well be thinking, "OK, that's an account of an astral encounter, but what is 'distinctly unusual' about it?"

I'll tell you.

When I awoke the morning after this 'dream' I was thrilled. I remember going over and over every detail of it in my mind, reliving it, and smiling. I **knew** it had been an astral encounter, and as the days went by and every particular remained perfectly defined in my mind, I counted myself blessed to have spent time with Harry again.

It didn't occur to me to mention anything about this to Carolyn. Although she was very interested in clairvoyance and mediumship as a result of her contact with Billy and me, it is probably fair to say 'the jury was out' in her mind as regards a great deal of subject matter that could fall under the umbrella of the Paranormal.

If I mentioned it at all, I decided, I'd just say I'd had a dream in which she featured.

A couple of weeks later Carolyn and I were due to go out together for dinner. She was picking me up, and arrived in her car outside the flat I was then living in.

I saw her out the window, ran down the stairs, and locked the front door of my building behind me. I walked over to the passenger door of Carolyn's Mini, smiling at her through the window. Once settled in the car we drove to a restaurant that we knew, parked, and made our way in, to a table.

We had been chatting the whole time since I had got into the car, and only paused now to take our coats off.

I noticed the scarf Carolyn was wearing – it was the one she'd had on in the astral encounter,

"That's nice," I said, indicating the scarf.

"Thanks," she said, "Mum gave it to me ages ago. This is the first time I've worn it. I feel a bit guilty really; I suppose I should have worn it before, but I'd forgotten about it!"

I smiled.

"I've got something odd to ask you," Carolyn said, looking almost serious for the first time that evening.

"Go on," I told her, "I'm all ears!"

"Well... Have you ever had a strawberry Mivi?" she said quietly; and I was aware of a faint note of anxiety in her voice. She leant towards me across the table, watching me.

I stared at her, wondering........

"Umm........ Why do you ask?" I said cautiously. I couldn't

quite believe what I'd just heard. Could it **possibly** be….?

Carolyn looked hard at me,

"It's just…….. I had this really vivid dream a couple of weeks ago," she said, "I can remember **all** of it now, all the details, it hasn't faded a bit like dreams usually do. Actually, it was more like reality somehow, rather than a dream …….." Carolyn paused, and took a deep breath, "and you and I were having strawberry Mivis!" she said, smiling but looking rather embarrassed, as if she thought I might laugh at her.

But of course I didn't.

"Were we with Harry?" I asked calmly.

"Yes!" she said, "How did you know **that**?"

"Where were we?" I asked, but I already knew the answer.

"On the sand dunes by the 'round house'," she said without hesitation, "I think I drove there."

We discussed our individual versions of our joint astral encounter, and discovered that they were almost identical, as you would probably expect.

Carolyn did not know what she had been wearing, and was amused to hear she'd worn the pink and grey scarf that her mother had given her,

"So this evening **isn't** the first time I've worn it!" she grinned, "I don't feel quite so guilty now!"

We both laughed about the strawberry Mivis. Neither of us knew if they were still on sale, or had been replaced by something more modern. It is certainly a very long time since I remember buying one or even seeing one.

Both Carolyn and I treasured the wonderful, exhilarating, joyful feeling we had both experienced at meeting and playing with Harry again, and to this day we both retain every clear, sharp detail of the encounter in our memories, and probably always will.

If proof were needed that we are able to leave our physical bodies via the vehicle of our astral bodies, and meet up with others who either continue to have a physical existence, or who have already completed it, then maybe this event goes some little way to providing that proof.

Chapter Six

Probably the most common sighting of a spirit, either human or animal, is the 'spontaneous' sighting, which by its very nature occurs when we least expect it.

It is that very spontaneity, the very unexpected nature of the sighting, that actually makes the sighting possible, and allows us to see the spirit.

In the course of a normal day, as we go about our normal material existence, we expect to interact with normal material situations, and with other people or animals that have a physical existence.

We think our usual thoughts; solve our usual material problems, and make our plans for a material future.

Throughout the course of a normal day we are habitually unaware of the use we make of our physical senses, for they fit us like a glove, and unobtrusively guide and protect us through the dangerous maze that is our physical existence.

We **expect** our physical senses to work for us, and we accept unquestioningly that they do. It is only when they do **not** work, and are thereby notable by omission, that we pay them any attention.

This is as it should be.

But we are not **just** a physical body with its set of corresponding physical senses. We are far more than that.

Simply put, we possess other, more spiritual bodies, each with their corresponding sets of spiritual senses. However, living as we do here in a physical world, those spiritual senses will maybe never be called into play, and never actually manifest.

Yet again, this is as it should be.

But allow your mind to wander without particular direction, during an excruciatingly boring meeting; lose your ability to concentrate on a difficult passage in a complicated book, and drift away; or allow your consciousness to wander freely as you stare fixedly at an object; and you thereby reduce the hold your physical senses have on you, leaving your more spiritual senses free to manifest, albeit unbeknown to you, to some greater or lesser extent.

Your 'guard' is lowered, so to speak, and given the right circumstances this is the moment when you may just see a spirit.

However, the unexpected nature of a spontaneous spirit sighting often results in the 'just my imagination playing tricks' response to it, and I am absolutely certain that very many people have actually seen a spirit, and disregarded it.

Sometimes the shock of seeing an unfamiliar figure in a totally unexpected place will instantly revitalize and reawaken the dulled physical senses, thereby suppressing the spiritual senses, and instantly removing our ability to continue to see the spirit figure. It seems to us that the spirit simply vanishes before our very eyes. And yes, it does indeed vanish, as our eyes 'retune' to our physical world, to the exclusion of anything from a more spiritual dimension.

We very often think we see dark, shadowy, half formed figures out of the corner of our eyes, catching us unawares while we are concentrating on something, or maybe just daydreaming; but then, when we quickly turn our gaze towards the spot to check it out, there is nothing there, or rather, nothing that we can see. We habitually put these experiences down to our over active imagi-nation, or a trick of the light. Indeed, this may well be the case most of the time. But then again, some of these figures, though barely glimpsed, fleeting and shadowy, may possibly be sponta-neous spirit sightings, which vanish from our view the instant we become aware of them.

It is worth mentioning here that there would appear to be a certain amount of confusion regarding the difference, if indeed any, between a 'spirit' and a 'ghost'.

We have all heard the stories about, for example, the ghostly horse rider galloping on his magnificent black steed over the bleak moors every full moon; or the ghostly corpses that swing from creaking ropes on the old oak at the crossroads when the daffodils bloom; or the young hitch hiker who suddenly runs across the narrow country lane in front of a car, in the early hours of a summer morning; or the platoon of Roman soldiers clad in fighting gear that marches past and through the old city wall in Chester; the list goes on and on……..

This type of story is well known. The theme is repetitive in nature i.e. the principal documented actions are constantly repeated in exactly the same way, maybe annually, maybe every five years, maybe at the full moon; usually at the same time of day or night, or in the same season, certainly in the same place.

These ghostly manifestations are in fact 'replays' of an event that once happened, projected onto a psychic 'screen', and visible to all who witness it. We are seeing into the past, very often hundreds of years back.

The 'actors' in these ghostly manifestations can no more see us than can an actor in a play on TV. For it is their **image** that we see, no more than that, recorded in every detail for posterity.

And this is the crucial point – a ghost is not an entity which has an existence; it is a 'picture' or 'vision'; a recording of an entity which **had** an existence in the physical world, and which was in some way involved in an event so traumatic, so horrifying, so emotive as to cause a veritable outburst of emotion strong enough to in some way imprint the event itself on the aether or psychic space within which we have our existence.

And there it will remain, like a CD or DVD filed in a library, until such time as it is triggered into a replay, a rerun of the event which caused it to be created in the first place.

It goes without saying then that there can be no meaningful interaction between a 'ghost' and ourselves. The ghost is as unaware of the wider surroundings within which it appears, as is the actor in a TV film playing in your living room.

But a 'spirit person' is just that i.e. a person who has completed a corporeal existence and has moved on into a new form of existence in the Spirit World, discarding the physical body, whose usefulness is now past.

Despite the difficulties and complications of spirit communication there can be, and often is, meaningful communication between those who live on in the Spirit World, and those of us who still have a physical existence here in the material world.

Julie is a friend of mine. Although she is obviously aware of what I do, and what my lifelong interests are, we very seldom discuss psychic and spiritual matters, and have only very infrequently, in all the time I have known her, touched on the subject of an afterlife.

This is not actually all that unusual, as I do not tend to 'talk shop' with my friends, and prefer rather to leave those subjects to within my private readings.

An animal lover, with a little flock of ex battery hens, several dogs and cats, and a really busy life, it is probably fair to say that Julie is healthily skeptical where Spiritualism and matters of the Paranormal are concerned, although she would be the first to admit that her working knowledge and experience of both areas is actually extremely limited. However, it is certainly true to say she is nobody's fool.

Not long ago Julie went round to a friend's house for coffee and a chat. She has known Pat for many years, and quite often drops in to see her in the large, old Victorian house where Pat lives.

Since Pat's parents had retired they had been abroad several times, making the most of their well deserved retirement. They kept themselves busy with a number of interests and pastimes at home too, and Pat used to joke that she saw a lot more of them when they were both working.

But Pat was pleased for them, and only too happy to look after Sophie, their much loved, beautifully natured, elderly dog, while they were away. Pat's house was Sophie's second home, and she loved coming to stay almost as much as Pat loved having her.

The arrangement suited everyone.

On that particular day Pat made coffee, and she and Julie settled down opposite each other at the round, wooden kitchen table for a good natter, as they had done many times before.

It was a spacious room, with a high, airy ceiling and old, polished wooden floorboards, which creaked comfortably as you walked over them, as befitted a wooden floor in any Victorian house.

Julie sat with her back to the window, in her usual place. It was a bright day; the rain of the morning had washed the clouds away, and now the sunshine was unbroken, though not strong enough at this time of year to remove the damp chill from the air.

But Pat's kitchen was warm and welcoming, and Julie took off her jacket, reached round and draped it over the back of her chair.

Pat was telling Julie a complicated story about one of their mutual friends, the ins and outs of which necessitated a fair amount of concentration on Julie's part.

As she turned back towards the table, and reached out to pick up her coffee cup, Julie noticed a movement in the open kitchen doorway, behind Pat.

Sophie was standing there looking round, as Julie had seen her do countless times before. Her sandy colored, curly fur caught the sunlight shafting through the window, and glinted dully. She took a couple of steps into the kitchen and stopped, looking over towards Pat, her head slightly tilted to one side, as if listening to something that only she could hear.

Julie smiled. She hadn't known that Sophie was staying at Pat's that week.

She made a quick mental note to tell Pat how well Sophie was looking for her age, and then dutifully refocused her attention on Pat and on the complicated story she was still telling.

Having finally finished what she wanted to say, Pat moved on to talk about other things, with barely a pause in her delivery. The two friends chatted for quite some time, and then Pat stood up to make them another cup of coffee.

A companionable silence fell on the kitchen. The sound of the kettle boiling seemed suddenly very loud,

"I've got some bad news I'm afraid," Pat said, as she poured boiling water into the cups, and jangled the spoon around, stirring the milk in, "Sophie died last week."

The words hit Julie like a sledgehammer, coming as they did totally out of the blue. She was stunned into complete silence.

Pat walked over, put the cups of hot coffee gently onto the table and sat down again,

"She was thirteen, you know," she said quietly, "that's very elderly for a dog. But she went peacefully, in her sleep," she sighed, "Mum and Dad are devastated."

And, her mind elsewhere, Pat raised her cup of coffee to her mouth, realized it was still too hot to drink, and placed it carefully back on the table again.

A thoughtful silence settled between the friends.

Julie decided not to tell Pat that she had seen Sophie no more than thirty minutes ago. She decided not to mention that the little dog had walked into the kitchen and looked around.

Her decision was based on the fact that Julie herself could not understand what had happened. She **knew** without a doubt what she had seen, but she didn't know **why** she had seen it, or **how** it was that she had seen it.

This is a wonderful example of a spontaneous spirit sighting, coming as it did to someone who was not in any way predisposed to seeing spirit; someone with no 'track record' where this kind of thing is concerned, and of course to someone who was not even aware that Sophie had died.

During the last eighteen months of his life my father came to live with me. My mother had died the year before, and Dad, his health failing, was struggling to cope alone.

Because of our past, unhappy history I wasn't sure I would be able to look after him; I wasn't sure I would be able to care for him in any meaningful way. Although we had 'reconciled' in latter years, we had done that by simply never mentioning the awful, loveless period of my life which had been my childhood, or my father's part in it.

While my mother was alive we had her in common, and never needed to spend too much time alone in each others' company. Awkward questions never arose, and potentially awkward situations were easily avoided.

The day that Mum told me, shortly before her death, that she was worried about what would happen to my father when she died, I told her that I would look after him. My words carried a conviction that I did not feel, and hung uncertainly in the air between us. I will never forget the look she gave me.

I believe she thought I would certainly **try** to care for my father, but I'm convinced she felt I would not be able to do so, that it would be beyond me, and that the sad and bitter resonance of the past would prevent me from carrying out my promise to her. That look reflected a hundred different and conflicting emotions in turmoil, and will stay with me forever.

But later, as my father and I moved with slow, tentative steps away from being almost complete strangers with an intense dislike of each other, towards something akin to feeling at ease in each others' company, he began to open up and speak to me, to tell me wonderful, interesting, amusing, and for me undreamed of things about his childhood, and about family members whose names I had not even heard mentioned before.

I am so very glad that he did, for my father gradually became a person to me; sentient, and possessing a soul. That hard, unyielding sheaf which had always been tightly wrapped around him where I was concerned started to break down and fall away, and I began to know him in a way I had never thought to know him. I realized that there were other, hitherto hidden and unsuspected sides to my father's nature, and that he had a dry, wry sense of humor.

Little by little it became evident to me as I listened to him speak, that my father himself was fey. I suppose I should have expected that, given the strength of his mother's clairvoyance.

This is one of the stories that he told me:

As a child growing up in the Liverpool of the 1920s my father was no different from any other youngster of those uncertain times following the First World War.

His father, and most of his numerous, young, fun loving uncles on his mother's side were already, or were shortly to become sailors.

Between them, with their combined wealth of nautical knowledge, they could probably have crewed and sailed just about any ship of the time, spread as they were between ships engineers below deck, and officers and crew above deck.

There was never any doubt that my father would follow in their footsteps, and make the sea his life.

Both his father and mother had been born in Scotland, and came from old Scottish families who could proudly trace their pure Scottish ancestry back many generations. Both families had relocated to Liverpool in search of seafaring work with the big shipping lines that were then based in that thriving city.

In his childhood years, before he joined the naval training ship Conway and left Liverpool, my father spent a great deal of time with his maternal grandparents, at their noisy, chaotic home not far from Liverpool city centre.

Dad's mother was one of twelve children, mainly boys, and as she was the first born, several of Dad's uncles were not that much older than he was.

That of course made for wonderfully fun visits to the rambling old house, with frequent hush hush 'meetings' in the dilapidated outhouses while his uncles smoked their illicit cigarettes;

marvelous and scary games of hide and seek through the dark, narrow, wood lined corridors of the old house; mad games of chase with the family dog up and down the two long staircases; and free front line seats at the window on the top floor for the cricket matches that happened nearly every week at the rather prestigious cricket club opposite the house.

Dad remembered his grandfather as a slender, quiet, softly spoken, elderly man, who spent most of his time sitting at the kitchen table reading a newspaper or a book, while happy family chaos raged all around him. He appeared oblivious to the children's loud voices and frequent arguments, to the sudden games of catch the ball that would break out around and over the table, and to his wife's oft repeated plea to move to another chair while she cleaned around him.

Dad loved his grandfather dearly, and his grandfather loved him.

One day Dad was sitting next to his grandfather reading the newspaper that was spread out on the kitchen table in front of them both. The house was surprisingly quiet; it was a Saturday, and most of the children were off somewhere doing the usual important Saturday things.

After a while the old man leaned back from the table, and slowly reached into the front pocket of the waistcoat that he always seemed to wear. He took out his gold pocket watch, pressed the screw on the top of it with his thumb, and squinted down at the watch face now revealed by the opening of the watch's hinged front.

Dad glanced in his grandfather's direction, and caught sight of the beckoning motion of the old man's hand towards him, as his grandfather slowly stood up and moved in the direction of the kitchen door, returning the pocket watch to its habitual place in his waistcoat as he went. Dad jumped up and followed his grandfather, aware that his grandmother, standing at the sink, had stopped washing dishes and was watching the pair of them in silence, a half smile on her face.

Walking slowly along the hallway and pausing at the bottom step of the first of two steep staircases in the house; his grandfather turned to Dad and, in his soft, broad Scottish accent said,

"You run on up to the very top floor, and put a stool there by the landing window. You're just a wee lad, and you'll get up there faster than me," and he looked down at Dad, with a smile that spoke of conspiracies and shared secrets between them.

Dad had been sitting on the stool by the landing window waiting for his grandfather for quite a few minutes before he heard slow, heavy footsteps falling on the threadbare stair carpet, accompanied by the steady, labored breathing of a gentleman whose health had seen better days.

When finally his grandfather was settled on the stool, and his breathing had regained a semblance of normality, Dad said,

"What are we doing up here Gramps?" and he looked around at the small, dingy landing with just one door off it, as if he might find a clue somewhere, to answer his question.

This was Barbara's room up here, tucked away at the very top of the old house; silent and secluded, far from the ubiquitous mayhem that reigned downstairs.

Barbara was one of only three girls in the family. Quiet and refined, amusing and affectionate, Dad thought the world of his young aunt, and was devastated when she died as only a very young woman not many years later.

His grandfather didn't answer, but pulled the old wooden stool with the plaited rope seat nearer to the small, low landing window, and rested his elbows on the sill, staring out. Dad stooped and looked through the window, wondering what there was to see out there.

And so began what would become my father's lifelong love of the noble game of cricket, for the landing window afforded an uninterrupted view across the pitch and pavilion of the prestigious cricket club on the other side of the road.

From that moment on, whenever there was a cricket game, or team practice, Dad would sit glued to the window at his vantage point, usually side by side with his grandfather who, having been something of a cricket aficionado for many years, always seemed to know something interesting about most of the players, no matter which team. His softly spoken snippets of information reminded Dad of a radio commentary.

One bright spring Saturday Dad climbed quickly back up the two staircases to the top of the house clutching a cup of tea destined for his grandfather. He went as fast as he could without spilling the tea, not wanting to miss any of the cricket game which had been underway for most of the morning.

He set the hot cup down carefully on the edge of the window sill, and his grandfather reached over and picked it up almost immediately, smiling his thanks,

"They've done well, very well. Got more runs on the scoreboard than I thought they would," he said to Dad, "but they're all out now."

Dad looked across at the cricket ground where the players were streaming towards the pavilion like homing pigeons, the white of their cricket clothes standing out very bright and clean against the smooth, vivid green of the turf. The spectators were all on their feet applauding the efforts of their local team; and there were smiles on everyone's faces.

But one player was standing alone at the side of the half dozen wooden steps that led up into the pavilion. He was staring intently at the now vacated field of play, one hand on the cricket bat that stood upright on the ground next to him, his body leaning slightly towards it, the other hand resting on his hip. He wore his cricket pads, gloves and a cricket cap. It was a traditional cricket player's pose.

This man was a picture of concentration, and seemed completely unaware that all the other players had now disappeared into the pavilion for lunch, and he was left outside alone, obviously immersed in a world of his own,

"Who's that player still standing by the steps?" Dad asked his grandfather, and getting no response from the old man he pointed towards the solitary figure, "Which side is he playing for?"

"What's that lad?" his grandfather asked, getting up and stretching his stiff legs – they'd been sitting together at the window for nearly three hours, "I'm ready for my lunch," he said, "Come on now," and he moved slowly towards the top of the stairs, reaching out to grasp the banister rail to steady himself on the steep way down, Dad's question completely unheard and unintentionally ignored.

Dad looked out through the window again, but the solitary cricketer had gone. He gave the figure no more thought, picked up the half empty, discarded cup of tea that stood on the windowsill, and followed his grandfather back down the stairs and into the kitchen for lunch. By the time he got there he had completely forgotten about the player who had been standing alone by the pavilion steps.

Not long after this Dad was once again to be found in his usual place on the landing at the top of his grandparents' house, staring out the window at the cricket ground opposite. But it was pouring with rain on this occasion, and play had been postponed. They hadn't even been able to start the match as the massive, black storm clouds rolled in from the Atlantic on a shrill, persistent north westerly wind, and shed unrelenting rain over the whole of Liverpool.

His grandfather had sent him upstairs to see if there was a break approaching in the storm, or if it looked as if the worst was over. But from the window Dad could see that the sky was lowering, and the rain still fell in an almost solid curtain, only interrupted here and there by unpredictable squally winds.

The old eves on the house creaked and groaned, and the wind whistled and screeched around the loose roof tiles and gutters, rattling and wrenching at them, threatening to rip them off and smash them into pieces on the road below.

There would surely be no cricket played here today. Dad shivered; the old house was drafty and there was a dank chill in the air on the landing. He turned away from the window, but something caught his eye as he did so. He looked out again, towards the cricket field. There was something there, on the field, not far from the pavilion; he could just make it out through the driving rain that formed a sheet of moving water against the outside of the pane of glass, thus distorting all vision through it.

But yes, Dad could see that someone **was** standing there, unmoving in the pouring rain. He blinked, leant closer to the glass, and stared.

He recognized the figure as the same, solitary cricket player from a couple of weeks ago, and almost unbelievably, the man was standing in the same place as then, wearing his cricket whites, cap and pads, and leaning on his bat. He was not wearing a rain coat or holding an umbrella. As before, he was staring towards the cricket pitch.

A sudden deep peal of thunder from overhead made Dad jump. The storm seemed to be passing right over the house, and he looked up, hoping to see flashes of lightening through the clouds. He already possessed, at that young age, a mariner's love of and respect for the power of the elements, and enjoyed nothing more than watching a storm unfold or a strong wind rage.

Looking back towards the cricket ground some minutes later Dad could see no sign of the figure, or of anyone at all outside in the rain.

He went back downstairs to the kitchen and told his grandfather that there was as yet no end in sight to the storm.

The old man nodded, he had expected that. He threw some pieces of coal onto the open fire, the only source of heat in the kitchen, and then beckoned to Dad to sit beside him in front of the flames, where it was warm. They settled down together, easy in each other's company, and began to read their books.

But Dad could not concentrate; he could not erase the vision of that solitary figure from his mind. Why would anyone stand out in the pouring rain if they didn't have to, and without a coat?

Unable to keep this mystery to himself Dad told his grandfather about the cricketer, detailing the two occasions on which he had seen the man,

"I just wonder why he stands there on his own. It seems strange," he said.

"Well, they've got some real characters playing for them at the moment!" the old man said, chuckling, "who knows **what** they get up to!" and he shook his head, still smiling.

"But I don't think he's in the local team," Dad said, "I haven't seen him actually playing, either fielding **or** batting."

"Oh?" The old man raised his eyebrows, and thought for a moment, "You'd recognize him again, would you?" he asked.

"Yes, I think so," Dad told him.

"Then pass me those papers, and we'll see if we can find him for you," Obediently Dad stood up and walked over to the pile of newspapers his grandfather was pointing at. He carried them back to the fireside, and put them on his grandfather's knees.

The papers all contained articles and photos relating to cricket, mostly in and around Liverpool, and dating back a couple of years. The old man flicked carefully through the pile, extracting a paper here and there, and putting it aside. Eventually he had looked through them all, and turned his attention to those he had set aside, scrutinizing each page, looking closely at each photo.

Finally he handed a couple of newspapers to Dad, their pages open at photos of local cricketers facing the camera in a variety of poses; some group photos, some individual,

"You might see your man there, amongst those fellows," he said, leaning back in his chair and watching my father with interest.

But no, look as he might, Dad didn't see 'his' man in any of the photos, and was quite disappointed not to have located him.

"Well, if he isn't there that probably means he isn't a regular member of a local team. Maybe he just replaces a player who's ill or who can't play on a particular day...." his grandfather said. He thought for a moment in silence, then,

"What did he look like? Maybe I can do a bit of digging for you...." he smiled at Dad.

"Well, he had a big black moustache," Dad said, "that's why I'd recognize him again. I don't really know what his face looked like, and he had a cap on, so I don't know what color hair he had – probably very dark, like the moustache," and Dad grinned sheepishly, realizing that the only thing he knew for sure about the mystery cricketer was that he had a big black moustache.

"Well, that's something I suppose!" his grandfather said wryly, "I'll see what I can do for you."

Time passed. A couple of days, maybe a couple of weeks; Dad gave no more thought to the solitary figure he had seen on the cricket ground.

Then one day he ran round to his grandparent's house after school, and was surprised not to find his grandfather in his usual place at the kitchen table, or sitting in front of the open fire,

"He's in the box room dear, on the first floor," his grandmother told him, "and he's got something for you, so you'd better go on up there! But tell him tea is ready, so don't be long," and she smiled.

Dad ran along the hall and up the stairs, wondering what his grandfather was doing in the box room. It was small, dusty, and these days crammed full of things nobody wanted, but were loathe to throw away. Masses of old toys were piled higgledy piggledy in one corner of the room, and there was a bookcase full to overflowing with old school books and atlases against one wall. Dad had sometimes whiled away a rainy afternoon by trawling through the old, leather bound encyclopedias, looking for photos of sailing ships, and far away, exotic ports.

He found his grandfather sitting on the old stool just inside the box room door. He was surrounded by newspapers and magazines which were strewn untidily around on the bare wooden floorboards, making it appear that a tornado had passed that way. He was staring at a magazine in his hands, and had half a dozen more balanced precariously on his knees.

"What are you looking for Gramps?" Dad asked, peering round the door.

"Ah! Yes! Well, I've found something you might be interested in," the old man said, looking round at Dad and spilling the pile of magazines from his knees onto the floor, "Now, where did I put it?" and he began searching through a mound of jumbled papers piled at his feet, "It's here somewhere."

Dad tried to help, picking up and folding newspapers, some yellowed, torn and disintegrating with age, and smoothing them back into order in piles,

"Yes! Here it is," his grandfather said, pulling a magazine out from under the bottom shelf of the bookcase, "I put it here so I wouldn't lose it. I want you to have a look at it, you see. You may just recognize someone," and he passed the magazine to Dad.

There were a number of black and white photos on the double page spread, and they were all of cricketers. Some were standing in groups, others posing alone. The page headline read "Our Liverpool Cricketers" (at least that's what Dad remembered it read) and several clubs from the city were represented there.

Dad peered eagerly at each of the photos in turn, but although several of the cricketers had moustaches of differing shape, color and size, he couldn't spot the man he had seen on the field beside the pavilion.

"No, Gramps," he said, "he's not here," and he passed the magazine back to his grandfather.

"Try these," the old man said, turning over to the next page, and passing the magazine back again.

He was there. The cricketer who Dad had seen twice was there on the page, photographed with four or five of his cricketing colleagues, standing casually in a half circle, laughing towards the camera. Dad recognized him immediately,

"There he is Gramps! That's him," Dad said triumphantly, holding the magazine out so that his grandfather could see which cricketer he was pointing to.

The old man looked, and reached out and took the magazine, holding it up towards his face so he could see the photo more clearly in the dim light reaching in through the box room's small window. He didn't speak,

"Who is he?" Dad asked curiously, "Which team does he play for?" and he leaned across to look over his grandfather's shoulder.

"You're sure, are you?" the old man asked.

"Yes. Absolutely. He's leaning on his bat in the photo, the same as when I saw him; and you couldn't miss that moustache!" Dad said.

"Umm. You couldn't be mistaken, lad?" There was an odd, unfamiliar note in his grandfather's voice.

"No, that's him. I've seen him twice," Dad said, "Why?"

"Well........" the old man hesitated, laid the magazine down on his knees and looked at Dad, "It says here that his name is George Allenby*," he paused, still looking at Dad, "and he died four years ago."

In the silence that followed this disturbing revelation, the patter of the rain outside sounded very loud against the box room window. Dad moved uncertainly from one foot to the other, and back again, his mind racing. He couldn't think what to say; he didn't understand how he had seen George Allenby* out there on the cricket pitch. But he knew he **had**. He knew it.

"Come on then," his grandfather said, getting slowly to his feet, "I'll bet our tea is ready downstairs," and he put a gentle hand on Dad's shoulder, guiding him out of the box room doorway and onto the landing.

"But, what...why did....?" Dad started, meaning to ask his grandfather's opinion about this 'incident'; and why he thought Dad had seen the cricketer, a cricketer who had died four years previously. But before he could even formulate the question the old man turned to him and said,

"These things happen lad, these things happen. Who knows why," and he reached out and grasped the banister rail, and began to descend the steep stairs slowly and carefully, without another word.

Dad followed him.

The 'incident' was never mentioned again.

When Dad told me this story, so many years after the event, we laughed together. We wondered if his grandfather had told Dad's grandmother about it, and if so, had the old couple said something to each other along the lines of "Like mother, like son" and shaken their heads, wondering?

Probably.

* Dad could not remember the cricketer's name, so I have taken the liberty of making it up.

Chapter Seven

I always struggle to find suitable examples from my private readings which I can relate here in a book, without exposing the identity of the person or persons involved.

I am obviously looking for examples of readings which the book reading public will find of interest, but of course anything particularly unusual or in some way fascinating, or indeed anything at all which has occurred in a private reading should be just that – private.

So, once again I have changed names, occasionally genders, and some other pertinent details in the following examples, and hope that I may be forgiven for doing so.

The doorbell rang. My 3pm reading was exactly on time, as usual. I opened the door to Maggie, a surprisingly trendily dressed, though sophisticated middle aged lady who I had seen two, maybe three times before, over the course of a couple of years.

She came into the house amidst a flurry of windblown rain drops, apologizing for leaving her footprints on the tile floor of the hallway. We laughed. When you have a dog, as we do, there are usually any number of paw prints, or worse on the floor in wet weather, so one or two more prints of any kind made little difference.

I followed her into the front room and closed the door gently behind me, instantly grateful for the glow of warmth that washed over us from the wood burning stove. The day had turned distinctly damp and chilly, with the kind of chill that is hard to shrug off; it was a dismal chill, typical of autumn in the north of England, and one that seemed to invade your very bones.

Maggie shivered, smiled at me and took off her heavy jacket. She sat down on the couch, laying her jacket carefully alongside her.

I settled into my usual chair opposite the couch and looked over at her.

I didn't have to be psychic to see that all was not well with Maggie that day. She looked tired, and her mid length blond hair, usually so well styled, even glamorous, looked uncharacteristically untidy, as if she hadn't taken the time, or the bother, to brush it that morning.

I suddenly became aware of a disturbing, almost electric feeling of tension hanging over her, as if the unexpected addition of even the slightest problem in her life at this moment would just be too much for her to cope with, and would send her over the edge, into despair.

I wondered what had happened along her pathway through life to bring her to this point; what was it that weighed so heavily on her shoulders?

I smiled at her; a smile of what I hoped she would see as encouragement. She was fiddling with the gold rings on her left hand, turning them round and round on her fingers, probably unconsciously - a sure sign of nerves. I wondered again what was wrong. I had not seen Maggie like this before.

I began the reading, and my attention was instantly drawn to a pinpoint of bright white light floating in the air near Maggie's left shoulder. As I spoke it grew gradually larger, reaching somewhere around the size of the circumference of a football, glowing with a light so astonishingly bright that I was, as usual, amazed that it wasn't in any way harsh on the eyes, or difficult to look at. But that is the nature of a spirit light; heralding the appearance of a spirit person, and glowing with that other world brightness characteristic of another dimension, and never seen in the physical world.

Suddenly Maggie interrupted me, and in a rush, her voice breaking with emotion said,

"I'm so worried about my job. What's going to happen about

my job?" and she leant forward on the couch, her hands on her knees, staring intently at me, waiting for an answer; hoping for the **right** answer, the right answer being, of course, the answer she **wanted** to hear, maybe even **needed** to hear.

There was absolute silence in the calm, warm room. I looked at Maggie and saw the white knuckles of her clenched hands, and felt the turbulence of her emotion.

Any medium walks a thin line; a line fraught with potential difficulties and pitfalls, a line which is drawn between doing their job, and providing the help or advice that a client asks for.

The job of a medium is, of course, to provide evidence of the survival of death – no more than that.

But every medium works differently, gleaning their evidence and presenting it to the client in a variety of different ways, and from a variety of different angles. Every reading is different and unique, and as such may be considered an experiment.

A medium may achieve their contact with the Spirit World through clairvoyance – the ability to see spirit people; or through clairaudience – the ability to hear spirit voices or sounds; or through clairsentience – the ability to sense spirit people, or to sense any number of pieces of pertinent information that the spirit world may try to 'impress' on a medium.

The gift of clairsentience is perhaps the hardest to explain in any meaningful way to those who do not work mediumistically. It is something akin to picking the pertinent information out of the very air, or 'feeling' for example, the name and description of a spirit person, how they died, their address, the job they did, and their favorite color almost 'pressing into' your mind. A good clairsentient medium, given a good spirit contact, may glean a vast amount of highly detailed, relevant information in this way, but may not be able to tell you how that information was obtained, or where it came from. They may not know, or more often than not, may simply not be able to put it into words.

It is often through the use of clairsentience that some of the best results are achieved, and some of the strongest evidence of survival of bodily death is produced.

Some mediums are 'only' clairvoyant, some 'only' clairsentient, and some are 'only' clairaudient. But most, as you would probably expect, have a sometimes, though not always, confusing combination of all three gifts, although in vastly differing ratios. Working with these three route ways to the Spirit World combined can be difficult. This is why some mediums seem to work in a slightly chaotic fashion, and some of the information they give appears garbled and incoherent, although it may be, and often is perfectly accurate.

It is not, therefore, the job of a medium to look into the future. A medium is not, and should not aspire to be a soothsayer.

But there are, however, two vital points which should be mentioned in this regard:

The gift of clairvoyance takes two forms. It is primarily considered to be the ability to see spirit people, although these manifestations occur along a wide spectrum, and range from, at one end, a perfectly clear, visible and well defined sighting of a spirit, to a vague, undulating and nebulous form at the other.

But clairvoyance is also a much wider psychic gift, involving the ability to simply 'see' or 'know' something that other people cannot, and this is often taken to mean the ability to see into the future, or the past.

Very many mediums actually possess this form of clairvoyance, and will use it during their readings, alongside their other gifts. Seeing into the future gives rise to the temptation to foretell the future – so it is really no wonder that the general public are unsure exactly what a medium is, and what a medium does, or should do.

The second point is that during a reading it is highly likely that a spirit person, thrilled to be able to make contact with a loved one left behind and grieving in the physical world, will very often want to give comfort and reassurance to that person, and what better way to do so than to pass on details of future events looming in their lives.

So a spirit person may well want to tell their loved one not to worry, because they will find the right job, the right partner, the right house, and the missing bank book. The list is potentially endless. And the more pressing the perceived problem, the more insistent the spirit person will be, and the more difficult it becomes for the medium to resist the pressure to pass on the information, and 'tell' the future.

It is hard, oh so hard, to remove that element of 'fortune telling' from a mediumistic reading, and in fact most mediums do not entirely succeed in doing so.

As I looked at Maggie that day I heard a man's voice echoing from the Spirit World, telling me that she would soon lose her job. I ignored the voice. I wanted a much wider picture of what was involved there before I even contemplated telling her any such thing.

I tried to continue the reading, and concentrated on other visitors from the Spirit World, and other, happier information, but I began to see a disturbing picture of Maggie building in my mind's eye. She was sitting alone in a sparsely furnished room, in front of a panel of three judges, as if being tried for some misdemeanor she had committed.

Eventually I could no longer ignore this image which intruded on my train of thought, so I carefully asked Maggie if she could explain it.

Unfortunately she knew all too well what it represented, and told me that she would shortly have to appear before a disciplinary hearing concerning her job. She was convinced that she would be sacked, although through no fault of her own.

The vague outline of a spirit person had built up next to Maggie, in place of the bright spirit light I had seen previously. A man now appeared to be sitting next to her on the sofa. His form was ill defined and unclear, but I knew he was trying to communicate, although I was having great difficulty under-standing what he wanted to tell me.

I eventually established that this was a man called Dave, and he was Maggie's uncle. They had been great friends before he died, and he was very worried about her now. He wanted her to know that he was watching over her, and trying to make things better for her, particularly where her job was concerned.

I told Maggie as much, and on hearing this she began to sob,

"I wish he **could** help me now," she said, rooting through her handbag and pulling a tissue out, "I don't know what I'm going to do. I know I'll lose my job, and I don't know if I'll get another one.... What do you think? Do you think I'll find another job? What do you think is going to happen to me?" and she dabbed at the tears that fell, her eyes pleading with me to tell her that all would be well in her life.

Although now very distorted and indistinct I could again hear a voice calling from the Spirit World telling me that yes, Maggie would indeed lose her job.

I really did not want to tell Maggie that, but I suddenly 'knew' that she would only be unemployed for a short time, and would then find work again, albeit only temporarily. It looked as though she would then embark on a series of temporary employments, but employments nevertheless, and certainly better than nothing.

I looked at her and my heart went out to her. I wanted to help, so I made a judgment call,

"Yes, I think you **will** lose your present job," I said softly, "I see the door closing on you, and I see you out of work; but the only reason I'm telling you this is that I know you'll find something else pretty quickly. Turn over every stone and you won't be unemployed for long."

Maggie sat perfectly still and stared at me, digesting this information. She seemed calmer now, and took a deep breath,

"OK," she said, "I know what I'm facing. I feel a bit better now," and she smiled at me, "I can do this, I can find another job."

I carried on with the reading as the rain lashed against the window and the heavy, black clouds rolled overhead. Maggie put her jacket on before she ran down the path to her car. She waved to me as she drove off.

During the next month or so I often wondered how Maggie was getting on. I hoped she was working, I hoped she had found a good job, and I hoped the loss of her job in such an unhappy way had not been too traumatic.

Eventually Maggie came back to see me.

This is what she told me:

On the day of her disciplinary hearing Maggie was understandably nervous. However, resigned to the fact that the loss of her job was imminent, she had already begun looking for alternative work, had sorted out a new CV, and already sent out several job applications.

She felt very vulnerable and isolated during the hearing, and was glad it did not last very long. Asked to wait outside the room for a moment while the members of the panel discussed her case, Maggie sat miserably and uncomfortably on the only chair in the corridor.

After no more than a few minutes she was surprised to be called back into the room to hear the panel's decision, and braced herself for the bad news that she was certain would come. This was it.

But, far from the decision she was expecting to hear, the decision that would have seen her out of a job that very afternoon, the panel actually apologized to her for the trauma she had been put through, and told her she would be reinstated in her job with immediate effect, with no black mark at all on her employment record.

Maggie was stunned, and overjoyed. As she thanked the panel and left the room all she could think was, 'Fiona was wrong! She was wrong! I haven't lost my job. I don't need to look for another one!' and she walked along the corridor, down the stairs and into her office, a huge grin of delight on her face.

She sat back down at her desk and unpacked the bits and pieces that had collected in her drawer over the past few years, and which she had already packed into a couple of plastic bags, ready to take home when she left the office for good, 'But I'm not leaving,' she thought, 'Fiona was wrong.'

Exactly one week later, with no prior warning, the company that Maggie worked for closed down. All the staff, Maggie included, were made redundant.

As she finished telling me this tale I felt the urge to giggle, but resisted the temptation. I wasn't sure if amusement was entirely appropriate given the circumstances, but Maggie herself began to laugh, and I joined in,

"Oh no!" I said, "Poor you. That was really bad luck."

"I didn't know whether to laugh or cry when it happened," she said, "so I did both!"

"But you're working now, aren't you?" I asked.

"Yes," she said nodding, "this is my second temporary job since I was made redundant. It looks as if that's the way things are going now, but I'm happy enough. Actually, I'm quite enjoying the change. It's keeping me young!"

Chapter Eight

The attractive, smartly dressed young woman who sat on the sofa in front of me one bright spring afternoon appeared completely composed and at ease. But appearances can be, and often are deceptive. Judgments made on the basis of appearance alone can be fatally flawed. Who knows what goes on in a stranger's life?

I had never met Lynne before and knew nothing about her, her family, or the circumstances of her life. I did not even know her name. And I did not know that her husband, a relatively young man, had recently passed into the Spirit World until, that is, he communicated during the reading, and was able to pass on some good, evidential pieces of information, along with his love. He had arrived in the room before Lynne did.

During the reading John, Lynne's husband, thanked her for the way she had organized his funeral; he said he had loved it. She looked at me quizzically, eyebrows raised as I told her this, her short, stylish blond hair glinting as it caught the sunlight that shone through the window behind her,

"Was he there?" she asked doubtfully, staring at me.

"He certainly was," I told her, "Wouldn't **you** want to go to your own funeral? I know **I** would."

"Well yes, I suppose so!" she said nodding, "I've never really given it any thought! John's funeral was packed out; masses of people turned up for it. And you know, it was a really uplifting service, not at all sad or depressing like some funerals are; lots of people told me they thought it reflected John's personality," Lynne paused, contemplating the past , "I'm glad he thinks I did the right thing for him," she said quietly.

Every so often spirit communication is clear and flows relatively easily. But so many factors are involved in the business of communication that it is impossible to isolate just one or two of them, and either blame those factors for causing poor communication, or thank them for being responsible for enhancing the quality of the contact.

The attitude and energy which a client brings to a reading; the energy of the medium on that particular day; the environment in which the reading occurs; the expectations of the client; and crucially, the personal chemistry between medium and client, are all of paramount importance to the success or failure of a reading, and this list is by no means exhaustive.

But without a doubt we must add to this mix the energy and communicative ability of the spirit person around whom the reading may revolve. A number of factors may inhibit their ability to communicate clearly, such as for example, and typically, over enthusiasm. This can lead to a lack of focus in the reading, making it nigh on impossible for the medium to remain in control of the flow of information, and in all 'mental' mediumship **focus** is the name of the game. It is crucial.

The reading with Lynne's husband produced some clear, evidential information, and then he stepped back, making way for an older man who introduced himself as Lynne's father.

Passing into the Spirit World does not instantly equip us with a pair of angel wings, a halo, and an angelic personality. That which we have become during our life in the physical world is in large part how we remain in the Spirit World, warts and all.

We take over with us those qualities or flaws, those aspects of our personalities which cannot be bought at any price, and which we have developed during our incarnation in the physical world; be they good or bad, positive or negative, desirable or undesirable.

Why would any of our strongest personality traits suddenly vanish on passing into the Spirit World? Why would we suddenly become something that we are not?

Lynne's Dad had retained his vibrant sense of humor. He was thrilled to be able to make contact with her, and began to talk about the family, her mother, and Lynne's sons.

I became aware of a small dog running enthusiastically round the room and jumping up to greet Lynne; and then her father reached down and picked up a substantial black cat. He held the cat in his arms and told me to tell Lynne that they were all together.

As I passed this information on she confirmed that her father was an animal lover and prior to his death had owned a black cat and a small dog, both of which were now in the Spirit World with him.

I suddenly heard Lynne's father asking how 'Bunty' was, and thinking this must be a family member or friend I asked Lynne who it was. She stared at me, eyes wide,

"Who's Bunty?" I repeated, "Your Dad is asking how she is."

"Bunty's one of my cats," Lynne said smiling, "She was Dad's favorite, he adored her."

"He still does," I said, "but he's very fond of your sons too!" We both laughed.

I could hear Lynne's Dad talking about football, and in the background I could hear the unmistakable sound of a football being bounced on hard ground. This is the sound that alerts me to 'coaching' in one form or another, so I said,

"Your Dad's talking about football coaching, and he's telling one of your sons to get on and do it. But he's telling the lad to take care with his knee. This seems to be very important," and I looked at Lynne, wondering if she understood what her father was saying.

She did,

"One of my sons is training to be a football coach, but he's dislocated his knee. It's a bad dislocation and is still causing him problems, so obviously he's worried about his future in that kind of very physical work," she smiled, "But Dad seems to know all about it!"

We laughed,

"There's not much going on around the family that your father **doesn't** know about!" I said.

Towards the end of the reading Lynne's father laid two passports on the table in front of me. He told me she was going to Greece soon on holiday.

Lynne confirmed this information.

"There are two passports here," I said, "So I know you're not going alone!"

She smiled,

"I'm going with my sister. We're looking forward to it; a lovely break and a bit of continental sunshine!"

"Well," I said, "there's something wrong either with one of these passports, or with the flight tickets. I'm not sure what you Dad is telling me, but he's adamant that there's a problem somewhere with some paperwork to do with the holiday. He's tapping the passports with his finger, so I would assume the problem is there."

Lynne looked at me blankly and shook her head,

"I really don't think so," she said, "I've just renewed **my** passport, and my sister's isn't out of date. And I checked the flight tickets yesterday – they're fine."

"Humm, that's a mystery," I said, "Well, I can only tell you what your Dad is telling me, and that's to check the paperwork again. Something is wrong, and he feels you need to rectify it."

By the time the reading finished I had forgotten about passports and paperwork, and any potential problems connected with them. I said goodbye to Lynne and never gave anything which had occurred during the reading a second thought.

Time passed, maybe three or four months, and Lynne came back to see me. She brought the sunshine with her again – the day was bright, warm and uplifting, and my room was filled with summer light.

As she settled onto the couch Lynne said,

"Do you remember what my Dad told me about the

paperwork for my holiday in Greece?"

I didn't; so she reminded me what had been said during her previous reading,

"And I told you there didn't seem to be any problem," she went on, "because my sister's passport wasn't out of date, and mine was new. And the plane tickets were ok too, because I'd checked them," she paused, watching me.

"Yes," I said, "I remember now. Your Dad was convinced something was wrong somewhere. It seemed to be something to do with the passports. **Was** it?" I smiled, wondering.

"Yes!" she said, "You'll never believe it, but my sister had just renewed her EIHC," she stopped, realizing I was staring blankly at her. I didn't know what an EIHC was!

"European Health Insurance Card," she said helpfully, "it's a pretty important piece of paperwork and my sister had just renewed hers. When I got home after the reading with you I rang her, and told her what Dad had said. She was sure nothing was wrong, but she had a quick look anyway, and.... Although her Health Card had just been renewed, when she checked it over she saw that the wrong date had been stamped on it, and it was actually out of date **again**!"

"Oh, wow!" I said, "Clever Dad!"

"Yes! And the Health Card was inside her passport, so he couldn't have been more accurate," Lynne said.

It is sometimes surprising, maybe even disturbing, to realize just how closely the Spirit World seems able to scrutinize the details of our lives. However, this scrutiny, some may even say nosiness, is carried out with the best of intentions by those who have only our best interests at heart.

For why would someone who had loved and cared for you when they lived a life in the physical world not retain the same emotions when they reach the Spirit World? Of course they do; love, and the desire to look after the one we love, in any way we can, does not die.

Chapter Nine

My friend Carolyn recently found herself, through no fault of her own, in the unfortunate position of staring imminent joblessness in the face.

She was employed by a department of the public sector which was reorganizing and downsizing, and the particular office in which she worked was closing completely.

Carolyn is one of life's conscientious workers, with an ingrained sense of responsibility, and the specter of a period of enforced idleness did not sit well with her. She had begun turning over every stone, following up every lead, and dedicating herself to the search for another job, in a determined effort to avoid the looming dole queue.

For the very first time, hoping for some guidance, she came to me one winter's afternoon for a reading. The thin rays of a weak, depleted sun reaching through the window of my room barely provided enough light to see each other by, so I lit the lamp. It shed a welcome pool of golden light half way across the room, and brought the illusion of summer warmth with it.

I didn't need to be psychic to see how depressed Carolyn was about the situation in which she found herself; her facial expression and body language told me that and more. But she brought a grey cloud of worry into the room with her too, swirling around the upper part of her body, and her head.

We do indeed carry our woes with us, but we carry our good fortune and happiness around us too.

Most psychics and mediums will see or feel at least some aspects of the incredibly complex human aura that surrounds us, and will usually 'pick up' from it the predominant emotions of the client quite easily. The aura cannot lie, but it is important to note that a medium, clairvoyant or psychic **can** make a mistake, at the very least in the interpretation of the information they may glean from the client's aura.

Before Carolyn had even taken her coat off and settled herself on the couch I became aware of a spirit figure building up in a corner of the room. It was a woman, and I heard a soft, indistinct voice say, "Grandmother". I really hoped this early arrival from the Spirit World was going to be able to put Carolyn's mind at ease regarding her career.

I started the reading, and as I spoke the spirit figure moved slowly towards us and became rather more distinct, recognizable now as an elderly woman with neat, grey, wavy hair, wearing a classic pale blue cardigan, and a light colored skirt.

She had a very pleasant, though pale face, and looked to me as if she was wearing lipstick, and maybe face powder.

The force of the feeling she brought with her was overwhelming; her emotion was almost a living thing; I felt I could have reached out and touched it. Without a doubt she loved her granddaughter, and was thrilled to be able to make contact with her.

I described the woman to Carolyn as best I could and she recognized the figure immediately as her mother's mother. Grandmother and granddaughter had indeed been very close.

I had become aware of a strong and pleasantly floral aroma brought into the room by Carolyn's grandmother. I couldn't place it, although I knew it was a familiar scent. I suggested to Carolyn that it was perhaps rosewater, but I couldn't be sure. The moment I said this, her grandmother's hand reached out and dropped a beautiful, pink, perfectly shaped cut rose onto the table in front of me. I saw her hand clearly as she released the flower, and I smelled the rosewater again as it penetrated and perfumed the air around me.

"For Carolyn," her grandmother said clearly, and I had to try hard to stop my tears welling up as I told Carolyn what her grandmother had said and done. It was a truly emotional moment, and one which, probably because Carolyn is a friend, I felt myself drawn into.

Carolyn dried her eyes and then told me that the pink, cut rose brought to the reading by her grandmother was highly significant:

She and her mother had lived with her maternal grandparents when Carolyn was growing up. She obviously saw a great deal of the old couple, and grew particularly close to her grandmother.

The house had an attractive back garden which both her grandparents were very fond of. They enjoyed looking after it, weeding, tidying and planting flowers and shrubs, and were often to be found pottering around in the garden together when the weather permitted.

Their pride and joy, and the showpiece of the garden, was a beautiful pink rose bush. It had grown large and attractive over the years thanks to careful pruning, and delighted the old couple with its masses of perfect pink roses every season. Given the right temperature, and a suitable gentle breeze, the wonderful aroma of rose petal perfume would fill the garden on a spring day.

Following the death of her husband Carolyn's grandmother would cut the very first rose from the bush each year, and put it in a small vase beside her husband's photo. It brought her comfort, and was something she did without fail every year until her own death.

As spring approached, the first spring following her grandmother's passing, Carolyn's mother came in from the garden one day and said,

"The roses are in bud on the bush. I'll wait until the first one is just about open and then I'll cut it for Mum and Dad. I'll put it in a vase on the windowsill next to their photos," Carolyn nodded; it seemed an obvious thing to do, the right thing somehow.

A couple of days later Carolyn came downstairs into the kitchen and saw her mother pulling on her gardening gloves,

"Are you putting the bedding plants in?" she asked,

wondering if she should be offering to help.

"No, not yet," her mother said, opening a kitchen drawer and taking out a pair of scissors, "I'm going to cut the first rose. It'll be ready now," and she walked across to the door leading out into the garden, turned the key, and pulled it open.

The morning was surprisingly warm for that time of the year, and a gentle breeze brought a light draft of fresh air into the kitchen. Carolyn stood in the doorway and watched her mother walk steadily across the lawn towards the rose bush in the far corner of the garden. The sunlight threw dark, moving patches across the grass as the leaves on the shrubs and bushes in the garden borders broke its path, and split it into a hundred dancing shards.

Suddenly, unexpectedly, Carolyn's mother stopped. She stood unmoving a few feet in front of the magnificent rose bush, and seemed to be staring down at something on the ground, something that Carolyn couldn't see from where she stood.

Carolyn called,

"Are you ok? What are you looking at?"

There was no answer, and she felt a slight feather of foreboding touch the back of her neck as she watched her mother's immobile figure. What was she doing? What had she found?

Carolyn stepped outside and walked quickly across the lawn. She reached her mother's side and saw immediately what had captured her attention. A perfect pink rose, surely the very one that her mother had set out to cut, lay on the grass at the base of the rose bush.

Carolyn stooped and picked it up. It felt fresh; the petals were still firm, still in perfect shape, and the leaves along the stem had not yet begun to droop and wilt. The rose could not have lain very long on the grass.

But the startling thing about this discovery, the odd, disturbing and inexplicable thing, was that the rose had clearly been cut from the bush. It had not been broken by the force of the wind and torn from the bush; its stem had not been damaged or flawed in its pattern of growth, weakening it and leaving it susceptible to nature's heavy hand; no, the pink rose had been carefully, perhaps even lovingly **cut** from the bush.

Mother and daughter stared at each other. They were both thinking the same thing - had Carolyn's grandmother somehow managed to cut the rose from the bush, maybe in an effort to reassure them that she was alive, aware, and living on in the Spirit World? For this was indeed the very rose that, had she still had a physical existence, she would have taken from the bush and put beside the photo of her husband.

Smiling, wondering, Carolyn and her mother walked back together into the house and put the pink rose in a vase, and then put the vase on the windowsill next to the photos of Carolyn's grandparents.

So the pleasant aroma of rosewater, and the single, cut pink rose that Carolyn's grandmother brought for her during the reading were indeed significant, and left no doubt in Carolyn's mind that her grandmother had come to speak to her.

And, overriding those persistent, niggling doubts which exist unbidden in the minds of even the staunchest 'believers', often clad in the guise of 'common sense', Carolyn was now sure that her grandmother **had** been responsible for somehow cutting that first rose from the bush all those years ago; she felt it, she **knew** it, and this brought her comfort.

However, this particular visitor from the Spirit World was a very practical lady, and having greeted her granddaughter in a way which left as little doubt as possible as to her identity, she then moved on to the pressing problem of Carolyn's job prospects.

She wanted Carolyn to know that she would definitely get another job, and quite soon. I passed this information on and Carolyn said,

"Maybe she's talking about the job I've got an interview for next week? I hope so; it's a good job, I'd like it," and she smiled expectantly across at me, waiting to hear more.

"Well...." I said doubtfully, "do you know what; I don't think you'll get **that** job. It just doesn't feel right. I don't think that particular job is for you," and in the heavy silence that followed my words I was suddenly acutely conscious of the disappointment that Carolyn felt because of them.

"Why don't you think I'll get that job?" she asked quietly.

"It's certainly not because you wouldn't be good enough for it," I told her hurriedly but honestly, "it's just that your grandmother keeps talking about "a woman" being instrumental in putting you forward for **another** job, and she keeps repeating "81". I don't know what she means by that. Did your grandmother live at number 81? Or was she maybe born at number 81? Was she 81 when she died?" I was clutching at straws now, unable to elicit any further information from the Spirit World which might help to explain this insistence on "81".

Carolyn shook her head,

"No," she said, looking pensive, "I can't think what she means; '81' doesn't mean anything to me."

"Well, **if** I'm right, the number 81 must have some significance to the woman who will help you to get a job," I said, hoping I **was** right. I don't like uncertainty in a reading.

"It **is** a woman who has recommended me for the job next week," Carolyn said, "but you don't think it's the job for me....?"

Her question hung in the air between us for what seemed an age. I knew I had to be absolutely certain before I spoke.

"No," I said, "I'm sure it's not. Your grandmother has just told me that the job you get will come 'out of the blue', and will be a huge surprise to you. She keeps saying, "Soon, very soon," so I think we should give her the benefit of the doubt and believe her, because this is not a lady who wants to be contradicted!" We both laughed.

I carried on with the reading and Carolyn's grandfather and other members of the family came forward. They all knew about the new job that she would soon get, and they all wanted to congratulate her in advance.

As she was leaving later on Carolyn said,

"They'll all look pretty stupid if I **do** get the job next week, and there isn't another job!" We both giggled.

"Have a bit of faith!" I told her.

Two days later Carolyn opened a letter addressed to her which had been delivered to her house. It told her that a position had become vacant in a particular office, and that she had been recommended for the job. The letter asked her to go ahead and ring a telephone number in order to fix up an interview.

She read and re read this letter which had arrived out of the blue. She could hardly believe what was in it. When she rang me shortly after, I could practically **feel** the grin on her face,

"Let me know how it goes," I told her, "but you'll get it. This is the job your grandmother was talking about."

A couple of weeks later Carolyn rang me again. She had phoned the number on the letter, spoken to the office manager, and subsequently attended an interview. It had gone very well, and she was impressed with the set up in the business, and found the other employees very agreeable. She was sure that the position would suit her down to the ground.

"Well why are you sounding so glum?" I asked her, "Your life is just about to change for the better; the job is absolutely made for you, what more could you wish for?" I wondered what was wrong.

"Well, they practically offered me the job at the interview," she said, "and they promised to email me with definite proposals, but I haven't heard from them again. So maybe they've found someone else. Maybe my grandmother was wrong about this job."

"Don't be daft!" I told her, "Send them an email asking what the situation is. There's probably some simple explanation why they haven't been in touch yet. Believe me; your grandmother is **not** wrong!"

Carolyn was back on the phone to me the next day,

"I got the job!" she said, "I'm really happy about it!"

"Well done!" I said, "You deserve it!"

"Oh yes, I forgot to tell you," Carolyn said, "Do you remember that my grandmother said 'a woman' would put the job my way?"

"Yes, yes I remember that," I said.

"And she said that the number '81' had some kind of significance to that woman?"

"Yes," I said, "I remember," I wondered what was coming.

"Well, the business I'm going to be working for belongs to Jonathan Smith*, and his mother is a friend of mine. I haven't actually seen her for a very long time, but she knows what my qualifications are, and what experience I've had. And she knows where I've been working these past few years. So when Jonathan told her about the position he needed to fill, she realized that it would suit **me** really well. So she gave him my name and address."

"Ah!" I said, "So that's the 'woman' your grandmother mentioned, the one that recommended you for the job."

"Yes…. But!" Carolyn said, "Listen to this! Here's the punch line! And you couldn't make this up! Jonathan told his mother about the vacant position, and she gave him my name and address, **when they were attending a party for his mother's 81st birthday!**"

"Oh wow!" I said, laughing, "That's a good one!"

* I have not used his real name

Chapter Ten

I have often been asked if I **know** when someone is lying to me. Well, the honest answer to that is …. sometimes; though not always. It depends where I am and what I am doing at the time.

I will usually become aware of dishonesty during a reading, because at that moment I am working, and my psychic senses are 'switched on' and in 'aware' mode. As a consequence, everything to do with the client, every expression, every word, every gesture is hugely magnified and laid bare, and it is at this time that I would expect to become aware of any significant dishonesty, if that is, it has a bearing on the reading

Dishonesty carries its own distinctive color with it, and even a small lie will stand out quite noticeably, as it spreads its color through the perpetrator's aura.

It is a fallacy to believe that a medium or clairvoyant is **constantly** in contact with the Spirit World, and hears or sees spirit on a regular basis throughout the day and night; or that they constantly receive impressions or messages from another dimension. Life would certainly become excessively hard to handle if that were the case.

The medium who cannot, who does not know how to, or who is unwilling to 'close down' their particular gifts, is asking for trouble. It is unhealthy in the extreme to remain constantly in 'working' mode.

So as I go about my daily life, shopping in the supermarket, driving through the traffic, spending time with friends, I am as unaware of the psychic and spiritual realms that surround us as everyone else is, and my consciousness is firmly directed towards life here, in the physical world. That is how it should be.

The medium who gives a message from the Spirit World at the drop of a hat, or the clairvoyant who approaches an unsuspecting member of the public with news from long dead Uncle Fred, are doing their profession, the Spirit World, and themselves a disservice.

There is a time and a place for everything.

The elderly lady who stood on my doorstep one bright, warm, summer's day smiled broadly as I opened the door to her. I noticed immediately that she was clutching an umbrella,

"Do you know something that I don't?" I asked her, pointing to the brolly.

She smiled,

"The habit of a lifetime!" she told me, "Why change now?"

We both laughed.

I had never met this agreeable lady before, and obviously knew nothing at all about her. She was accompanied by a younger woman, and the two of them came into the house and closed the door.

"Would you mind if my daughter sits with me during the reading?" the elderly lady asked me, turning slightly towards her companion, "My memory's not as good as it used to be, so Janet may help me out if needed."

I didn't mind, and ushered them both into my room where we settled ourselves, ready to start the reading.

It was a very pleasant reading to begin with, as befitted a very pleasant client, who I will call Emily; and a number of 'visitors' from the Spirit World made their presence felt, bringing comfort and laughter with them.

Emily must have been in her late seventies. She was a softly spoken, quiet and conservative lady with a gentle, wry sense of humor. Her daughter Janet was something of a carbon copy of her mother and sat quietly listening with interest as the reading progressed, her younger, more agile memory for the moment not required.

A woman's voice suddenly called out, "Mother", very clearly, from the Spirit World.

I could not actually see the woman who had called out, but I knew that she was not Emily's mother. She was too young. The alternative of course was that this woman was addressing Emily as **her** mother.

I suddenly felt that this spirit woman, who had not been too long in the Spirit World, was very close to Janet, and I felt her urging me to say something, to tell Emily and Janet who she was.

As tactfully as possible I asked Emily if she had lost a daughter, and I was taken aback at the tone of her quick response,

"No!" she said sharply, "Certainly not."

I felt the need to try to explain my question, the question which had elicited such an unexpected response, so I told Emily that a woman, who seemed to be about the same age as Janet, was addressing her as 'Mother'.

"I have no idea why," Emily said in the same sharp, dismissive tone.

I looked across at her, and saw immediately that this well spoken, hitherto pleasant lady was lying to me. Her colors told me that. There was no doubt.

"Her name is Anna," I said, "She has just written it in the air in front of you. She feels sure that you know her."

But Emily just stared coldly at me. She did not respond.

The rest of the reading was very difficult. I certainly didn't have to be psychic to know that Emily wanted to get it over with and leave. But I didn't know why.

Later, I sat alone in my room and wondered what Emily had wanted to hide, and why she did not want to acknowledge the woman called Anna. Without a doubt she had recognized her. But why had she lied to me?

However, it was none of my business, so I put the incident to the back of my mind, and tried to shake off the vague feeling of depression and dissatisfaction that hung over me; the result and residue of an unsatisfactory reading.

I did actually catch myself thinking about Emily once or twice over the next few weeks, wondering yet again what had prompted her seemingly out of character reaction, and her lie. But I told myself that it wasn't my business, and I wasn't likely ever to find the answer.

So it was a complete surprise to open the front door a day or two later, and find Emily standing there.

"I do hope I'm not disturbing you," she said, "I wonder if I could have a quick word with you?"

"Yes, come in," I said, "I've finished work for the day," and I held the door open as she stepped into the hall. I noted with amusement that she had her brolly with her again, and I glanced up at the cloudless blue sky.

"I owe you an apology," Emily said without preamble, as she sat down on the sofa in my room, "and an explanation." She smiled at me.

"Well no, don't worry........" I began, but she shook her head at me,

"My behavior was very rude," she said, "and you deserve an explanation."

"Really," I said, "You don't have to tell me anything."

"But I want to," she told me, "because you have helped me to right a wrong."

I wondered what on earth she was talking about.

"Many years ago," Emily began, "when I was first married, my husband and I really struggled to make ends meet. He didn't have a well paid job, and I worked shifts in a bakery, and that wasn't well paid either. Neither of us had any close family who could help us out financially.

So when I fell pregnant it was like the end of the world...." She shook her head sadly, remembering back down the years, "We knew we couldn't afford children then, and I cried and cried for days.

Our options were very limited, but we decided to have the child adopted as soon as it was born; I eventually came to terms with that decision. But then when the day came, and I gave birth, it was twins! Beautiful little twin girls."

She paused, and I smiled at her, wondering what was coming next.

"I couldn't do it," she said quietly, "I couldn't part with them once I'd seen them, and my husband and I argued for days. He wanted them both adopted, but we eventually agreed on a compromise. We would keep one twin, and have the other one adopted."

I nodded. I was beginning to get the picture.

"I can't tell you how guilty I felt," Emily said, "just having to make the choice; which baby to keep and which one to send for adoption…. And the guilt and heartache has never really left me, throughout my whole life," she shook her head, her eyes filled with tears, and she reached inside the cuff of her coat for a tissue,

"I could never bring myself to tell Janet. I couldn't tell her that she's a twin and I separated her from her sister. And even later on, when she became an adult, I just couldn't tell her. I didn't want her to judge me, you see, I was afraid of what she would think of me. The more time passed, the more I told myself that it really didn't matter."

The tears spilled over onto her cheeks and she dabbed at them with the tissue almost absent mindedly.

"I never knew what happened to Anna – yes, that **is** the name I gave her, and I asked the adoptive parents to keep it – we never had any contact. You didn't in those days. You simply handed your baby over and prayed that it would have a good life.

So when you told me that Anna was in the Spirit World it came as quite a blow. You'd already mentioned earlier in the reading that there are twins in our family, and I was suddenly afraid you were going to tell Janet about Anna," she looked at me and smiled ruefully, "I didn't really understand what a medium does, you see, when I came to you for a reading. It was a bit of a shock," and we both laughed.

"But," Emily said, "I have now righted at least some of the

wrong that I did all those years ago. I have told Janet about her twin, Anna, and what happened when they were born. And do you know what; she was wonderful about it, so understanding, and that's probably a great deal more than I deserve."

"You really shouldn't be too hard on yourself," I said, "Things were different in those days – you didn't have much of a choice."

"Maybe not; maybe not," Emily said wistfully, "but I certainly think I should have told Janet early on in her life that she was a twin. Anyway, she's started some research to see if she can trace Anna's adoptive family. I'll let you know when she finds them."

As I showed her out that day Emily put her hand on my arm and said,

"Thank you. Things certainly happen in a mysterious way."

I couldn't agree more.

Chapter Eleven

In 2009 Tod (my husband) and I went to Nepal for five months.

We travelled to a small, remote village which clings to the side of a deep valley high up in the Himalayas of the Everest region of that country, not far from Everest base camp; and we went there to teach English.

Although well known as a trekking destination, and of course as the home of that mighty mountain Everest, the globe's highest peak, (known to the Nepalese as Sagarmatha), Nepal is actually one of the poorest countries in the world.

Its unstable and volatile political situation means that little or no government help is provided for the population who struggle, particularly in the cities, to cope with such basic problems as poor, sometimes dangerously unclean water supply, and constant, day-long electricity blackouts.

From noisy, crowded, manic Kathmandu we made the 8 hour, sometimes hair raising journey up into the Everest region by road and track, and then we trekked, slithered and scrambled down the valley, through the glorious rhododendron forest to the village of Salle, where I arrived sweatily breathless, with shaking legs that I knew without a doubt would not be able to carry me one step further.

By the time we staggered into the village in the silent darkness of a Himalayan night, we had learned several things. One of those things was that Nepal is a stunningly beautiful, though sometimes starkly bleak country, which can, and often does make you stop and gasp as you gaze at its astonishing vistas, knowing full well that you are standing just a breath away from the roof of the world.

Something else we had learned was that the people of Nepal are wonderfully warm and friendly, and possess on the whole a great sense of humor.

The villagers and children of Salle (pronounced Solley) did everything they could to make our stay in their village a happy and memorable one.

It was, in fact, a life changing experience for us on many levels, and we fell in love with the bright, happy children who spend nearly every waking hour outside in the fresh Himalayan air, playing games they have invented, with bits and pieces of stone or wood that they have found on the terraces that surround their village. No computer games for them, no television or DVD, no cinemas or shopping malls, no fashionable clothes or trainers, no make up........ The list goes on and on.

But the thirst for education, for knowledge in the widest sense of that word, is there, and the children will walk for miles to attend their schools; but only after they have helped at home with the animals, crops or wood gathering. Truancy is almost non existent. The children of the Everest region appreciate what their schools can do for them, and they do not take them for granted or abuse them.

We grew very fond of, and developed a great respect for the hardworking villagers of Salle, those adults who stand looking on at the crossroads of their country's precarious attempts to modernize, and to build a better future for their children.

You will find a full description of the time we spent in Nepal and Tibet in our books *A Beard In Nepal* and *A Beard In Nepal 2*.

Kalyani was the young headmistress of the village school where we taught English, and she had the job of looking after us during our stay in Nepal. We didn't realize at the time that her duties included keeping us safe from the unwanted attentions of visiting wild tigers, amongst other things. She spoke reasonably good English, which was just as well because **we** could not manage to remember more than a couple of Nepalese words in the right order, try as we might!

Kalyani has a great sense of humor, and so do we, although I must admit that 'sense of the absurd' was probably more appropriate most of the time in **my** case. I spent quite a lot of time falling and slipping on the steep mountain paths, or stopping to gasp, puff and pant as the debilitating effects of altitude took their toll on my struggling lung power.

Kalyani was wonderful. Nothing was too much trouble for her where we were concerned, and the three of us spent quite a bit of time wandering along remote mountain tracks singing snatches of 'Old McDonald had a farm', while we tried our best to answer her endless questions about the workings of the world outside Nepal.

We told her something about our lives in England; how we lived, where we went and what we did, always careful to be as tactful as possible – after all, this was a bright, intelligent young woman who lived and worked in one of the world's poorest countries, and whose prospects therefore appeared to be decidedly limited.

One early evening, after we had been living in the village and teaching at the school for about two months, Kalyani came to visit us, as she often did, in our room upstairs in one of the village houses. She brought us some Nepali tea. We sat down together and began to chat.

During the conversation I asked her about religion in Nepal. The majority of the population are Hindus, but Buddhism is also practiced in parts of the country, with the two religions existing happily side by side. These days there has even been a merging of the two in some areas, with the population practicing a kind of hybrid religious mixture. But we had seen little or no evidence of any religious practices in the village, or even in the wider area around it. I was curious. Where were the temples?

It was fascinating hearing her opinions on the religions of Nepal. But of course Kalyani wanted to know about the religions of the West, and asked us, amongst a veritable barrage of other questions, what **our** beliefs were. Nepal appears to be a very open and accepting country where religious beliefs are concerned and

I saw no reason to sidestep or otherwise avoid discussion of my own beliefs.

During the conversation I told her that I did 'readings', and began to attempt to explain what these 'readings' entailed. But interestingly enough Kalyani seemed to know already,

"Oh yes, Fiona!" she said excitedly, "You get information from the ancestors in the next world," and she grinned at me, seemingly familiar with at least part of the concept.

We chatted for a few minutes more and then she said,

"Please Fiona, do a reading for me?"

I was taken aback, and stared at her, momentarily at a loss for words.

"Please!" she repeated, settling herself more comfortably on the edge of the bed she was sitting on, and leaning towards me, "Just a little reading is ok," and she smiled her special 'Kalyani' smile that filled the room and was impossible to resist. I groaned inwardly. My mind was light years away from where it should have been if I wanted to even contemplate doing a reading. I had spent the last two months tripping and falling all over the steep, majestic Himalayas, eating a very restricted diet, and sleeping uncomfortably on a bed with wooden slats instead of a mattress - none of which was really conducive to the particular mindset that I needed to adopt in order to do a reading.

"OK," I said brightly, though very possibly misguidedly, "I'll give it a go. But don't expect miracles!"

I put one of the room's two wobbly wooden chairs in front of Kalyani, and sat down on it, wondering what on earth I was going to be able to achieve.

There was complete silence in the little room. The heat of the day had turned gradually into a chilly evening. I shivered. I was glad I was wearing my heavy fleece trekking pullover. Tod leaned over and pulled the small, rough wooden shutter across the glassless window next to me. It creaked loudly as it closed, and I smiled at him. At least some of the draft was now prevented from entering the room. I felt instantly warmer.

I took a deep breath and started the reading.

It was a purely psychic reading, without the benefit of clairvoyance, clairsentience or clairaudience. Without a doubt the Spirit World looked on in stony silence, and may very well have disapproved of my efforts; for they, like me, knew full well that a mediumistic reading was far beyond my grasp at that particular moment. There is a time and a place for everything.

Everyone is psychic to some greater or lesser degree, although the majority of the population going about their everyday lives will never recognize that fact. Our 'psychic selves' manifest in a variety of ways. As I have already mentioned in Chapter three, intuition is probably the best known psychic gift i.e. the feeling that we just 'know' something, that we are privy to some secret, but we don't know **how** we know it. Or, we may perhaps experience the overwhelming feeling that something or someone is not 'right', and this is often a feeling that is so sharp it just cannot be ignored.

A psychic will 'read' and attempt to interpret the information carried around us in our aura, and this information may relate to a person's past, present or future. All mediums are psychic, but not all psychics are mediums, so a **purely** psychic reading will, by very definition, have nothing at all to do with the Spirit World. Many mediums disapprove of psychic readings and in fact this debate, the psychism versus mediumship debate, has raged for many years.

I was able to tell Kalyani that evening that she would not be living in the village for much longer, and that she would soon move to, and settle in a big city. She would not be teaching for much longer either, although she may return to that profession at a later stage in her life.

I told her that I felt she would soon do a lot of studying, and be successful with it.

Kalyani loved the reading! She began to ask question after

question, and giggled at the answers I gave her.

There was to be the birth of a baby somewhere very close around her over the next year; and finally, Kalyani would 'agree' something important with her boyfriend in the near future.

She raised her eyebrows at this piece of information. The boyfriend in question was studying in Australia, and wasn't due to return to Nepal for another couple of years at least,

"What does that mean Fiona?" she asked, looking puzzled, "What about my boyfriend?"

I shrugged, "Wait and see!" I told her, smiling.

Later on that evening, when the shadows were darkening and Kalyani had left, Tod said,

"What was that about her 'agreeing' something important with her boyfriend? Sounds a bit strange."

"Yes," I nodded, "I thought I'd better not tell her she's getting married soon!"

"But he's in Australia!" Tod said.

"I know," I said.

It was an odd place to do a reading, high up in the Himalayas, almost within touching distance of the mighty Everest; in a small, isolated village which had existed there, practically unchanged in every way, for many hundreds of years. The goats bleated and pulled at their tethers on the flat area of hardened clay outside the house, and the chickens scratched hopefully and noisily for seeds in the undergrowth on the steep terrace.

Over the months we grew used to the sounds of the village and the valley, but I know I would never have grown used to doing readings there!

Six months after we had left the village and returned to England Kalyani also moved away from Salle. She left the village and the school, and moved to Kathmandu. There she settled in a house with her boyfriend's sister in law, and enrolled on a computer and English language course at college.

Not long after, her boyfriend came back to Nepal for a short visit, and Kalyani and he were married. He then returned to Australia.

Kalyani's sister, with whom she was, and still is very close, had a baby at about that time.

During our stay in Salle we travelled back to Kathmandu several times, and also managed to fulfill a lifelong ambition of mine to visit that mysterious and intriguing country, Tibet. It was our good luck that its borders, hitherto closed to all comers, opened to foreign visitors while we were in Nepal.

We drove to Tibet along roads higher than the clouds, roads that clung to the edges of the rugged, steeper than steep mountains seldom seen by any Westerner; and we marveled at the vast, astonishingly silent, flat floored valleys that criss crossed the roof of the world.

The temples we visited, the monks we met, and of course the amazing Potala Palace, seemingly carved into the very mountain side, will forever remain in our memories. (There is much more detail in 'A Beard In Nepal').

Each time we went travelling the villagers would either make garlands of flowers to drape round our necks, or give us bunches of freshly picked flowers to take with us. This beautiful tradition is a centuries old way of wishing the traveler good luck, blessings, and a safe journey. It is of course bad manners to refuse to take the flowers, and anyway, why would you do so?

One day Kalyani, Tod and I set out to climb up the steep mountainside behind the village, to the rough track at the top, where we hoped to meet up with, and get a lift in a truck that was going to another village. From that village we assumed we would be able to get a mini bus to Kathmandu.

It was hot, and I struggled with a heavy backpack, but eventually reached the track and was glad to sit down at the side of it to wait for the truck.

A couple of villagers had noticed us, and they spread the word that we were setting out on our travels again. Pretty soon half a dozen village ladies arrived with flower garlands and bunches of fresh flowers for us. They walked along the track above the village, laughing and talking, looking lovely in their bright traditional clothing, until they reached us. Then they gave us their blessings and pressed the flowers into our hands. We were touched and thanked them very much.

Suddenly we heard the roar and screech of a vehicle's engine laboring down the track towards us, and a massive open backed truck, slewing unsteadily from side to side on the thick clay soil, rounded the sharp bend and stopped in front of us. We could feel the heat radiating out in invisible waves from its overworked engine.

We clambered into the back of the truck, threw our rucksacks into a corner, and settled down for what would be a very bumpy, dangerous, but exceedingly exciting journey.

But before the truck got under way we saw a figure in the distance, coming towards us along the track. The little gaggle of village ladies, who stood waiting to wave us off, turned and called to the newcomer, urging her to hurry. We saw her wave in response, and saw she was carrying a bunch of flowers. She tried, but she was elderly and couldn't walk any faster. She was still some distance away when the truck engine roared into life again.

Kalyani called to the driver to wait a moment, but her voice was lost in the din from the massive engine. She hammered on the top of the truck cab, but that too failed to attract the driver's attention, and now the truck began to move off down the track.

We stood at the back, helpless, hanging on to the tailboard, waving to the old lady. She was near enough for us to see her face clearly, and she was smiling, her long grey hair pulled back, and her red pashmina across her shoulders. She waved to us, calling blessings to us, the bunch of freshly picked flowers which had been intended as a gift for us still clutched in her hand.

We descended the steep mountain side in a series of bone

jangling bumps and crashes, and very quickly lost sight of the villagers who had come to see us off. But we knew who the elderly lady was, and we were very sorry to have missed her. She was the oldest lady in the village at 101 years old, and was much loved and respected by everyone. Her house was one of just a few situated on the steep mountain side up above the village.

After a journey fraught with unexpected difficulties, including a landslide which blocked the road, we reached Kathmandu. The image of the old lady trying to reach us, to give us flowers and blessings, stayed with us. We felt guilty that we had not been able to stop the truck, and that her efforts had been in vain.

"Don't worry Tod and Fiona," Kalyani told us, "When I go back to the village I will tell her that you are sorry. She will understand. She is a very kind lady."

Some time later, maybe a couple of weeks, Tod and I returned to the village of Salle. It was early evening when we arrived there, and we were tired from the journey. We climbed the old wooden ladder up to our room and, dumping our rucksacks, sat down on the 'balcony' outside. The amazing view out across the calm, silent, evening valley captivated us yet again, and we sat together in contented silence. The valley wall on the far side was covered in uneven terraces of different shapes and sizes, looking somehow like a series of badly made steps running down to the unseen valley floor below. Towering over the whole scene was a breath-taking, rugged snow capped mountain range, thickly forested as far up as the snow line.

I eventually stood up and went into our room to find a book, meaning to take advantage of the daylight that remained. I found the alternative, reading by candle light, difficult.

As I rummaged through piles of clothes and sleeping bags, trying to locate the book I wanted, the sudden, soft sound of a regular drum beat reached my ears from somewhere outside. I shivered. It was a haunting sound.

Clutching my book I rejoined Tod on the balcony. The sound of the drum beat echoed eerily across the valley, somehow accentuating the silent stillness that hung over the scene, and reminding us how isolated we were in that far flung place.

We knew that the drum beat was part of shamanic practice; we had heard it in the valley once or twice before. And Kalyani had told us that the Buddhist priests beat a drum, sometimes for 24 hours or more following a death, but we knew little more than that.

The mournful sound seemed to be coming from somewhere above the village, away to our left, but we couldn't see the source of the sound, and there was no one around to ask about it.

I settled down to my book, and pretty soon the drum beat drifted to the back of my consciousness and I no longer noticed it.

Some time later I got up and walked into our room to find the water. We had to use water filter bottles all the time to ensure that the water was safe to drink, and I had left mine in my rucksack. When I found it I realized it was nearly empty, so I began to fill it up from a plastic water bag containing local water. The bag hung against the wall on a nail where we had placed it two weeks previously, following our latest trip down to the local stream. My filter bottle would take just fifteen minutes to render that water safe to drink.

I was in the middle of doing this when Tod put his head round the door and said,

"The oldest lady's coming. She's just on her way down the path," and he beckoned to me to follow him outside onto the balcony.

"She's bringing some more flowers for us," he said over his shoulder in my direction.

By the time I stepped outside Tod was leaning out over the balcony looking left, up towards the steep, overgrown path that wound its way down to our house from the top of the village.

I joined him, expecting to see the old lady emerge from the path onto the wide area of flat, compacted clay in front of the house. But there was no one in sight. Everything was very still and quiet. Not a breeze stirred the vegetation; not a movement touched the tall corn crop at the side of the house.

The continuous soft beat of the drum still hung eerily over the valley in the twilight.

I looked at Tod. He shook his head, puzzled,

"She was almost at the bottom of the path," he said, "just over there."

"I wonder where she went?" I said, "Maybe she was on her way to some other house?" but we both knew that wherever her intended destination, she would have had to pass by our house, whether in front of it or behind. Either way we would have expected to see her.

"She waved at me," he said quietly, "I'm sure she was coming to see us."

But, although we waited on the balcony until the evening shadows had lengthened into darkness, the old lady did not appear.

Later, I awoke in the early hours of a Himalayan night and lay staring into the gloom that filled the room.

The now familiar, absolute silence that habitually engulfed the night time valley was broken by the continuing soft, regular beat of the drum. The eerie, mournful sound continued without a break throughout the night and into the next day.

We set off the following morning in bright sunshine to walk to the school. As usual we called at Kalyani's house to collect her.

"Why is the drum beating?" I asked her when she came out, ready to go.

She looked up towards the sound, towards the track at the top of the village, and shook her head. She looked sad,

"The drum is beating for the oldest lady in the village. She died yesterday," Kalyani said quietly.

Tod and I stared at her.

"I told the lady that you were sorry to miss her when you went travelling," she said, "and she understood. She sent you her blessings," and Kalyani smiled at us.

"When did she die?" Tod asked, voicing the question that was uppermost in my mind too, "What sort of time?"

"Yesterday morning," Kalyani told us, "while the sun was shining. After a death, when the priest comes, the drum begins to beat to help the spirit to make its journey to the next world. And because she was so old, and well respected, the drum will beat for her for three days."

Without a doubt the drum had already begun to beat when Tod saw the oldest lady coming down the mountain path, bringing fresh flowers for us.

Details of all Fiona Roberts' books can be found at:
www.spanglefish.com/fionaroberts

6th Books investigates the paranormal, supernatural, explainable or unexplainable. Titles cover everything included within parapsychology: how to, lifestyles, beliefs, myths, theories and memoir.